OPPOSING
VIEWPOINTS®
SERIES

Bankruptcy

Other Books of Related Interest:

Opposing Viewpoints Series

American Values

Corporate Social Responsibility

Government Spending

Poverty

At Issue Series

Poverty in America

Should the Rich Pay Higher Taxes?

The Wealth Divide

Are Government Bailouts Effective?

Current Controversies Series

Poverty and Homelessness

The Wage Gap

Social Security

"Congress shall make no law ... abridging the freedom of speech, or of the press."

First Amendment to the US Constitution

The basic foundation of our democracy is the First Amendment guarantee of freedom of expression. The Opposing Viewpoints series is dedicated to the concept of this basic freedom and the idea that it is more important to practice it than to enshrine it.

Bankruptcy

Noah Berlatsky, Book Editor

GREENHAVEN PRESS
A part of Gale, Cengage Learning

GALE
CENGAGE Learning·

Farmington Hills, Mich • San Francisco • New York • Waterville, Maine
Meriden, Conn • Mason, Ohio • Chicago

Patricia Coryell, *Vice President & Publisher, New Products & GVRL*
Douglas Dentino, *Manager, New Products*
Judy Galens, *Acquisitions Editor*

For more information, contact:
Greenhaven Press
27500 Drake Rd.
Farmington Hills, MI 48331-3535
Or you can visit our Internet site at gale.cengage.com

For product information and technology assistance, contact us at

Gale Customer Support, 1-800-877-4253
For permission to use material from this text or product, submit all requests online at www.cengage.com/permissions

Further permissions questions can be emailed to permissionrequest@cengage.com

Articles in Greenhaven Press anthologies are often edited for length to meet page requirements. In addition, original titles of these works are changed to clearly present the main thesis and to explicitly indicate the author's opinion. Every effort is made to ensure that Greenhaven Press accurately reflects the original intent of the authors. Every effort has been made to trace the owners of copyrighted material.

Cover Image ©zimmytws/Shutterstock.com.

LIBRARY OF CONGRESS CATALOGING-IN-PUBLICATION DATA

Bankruptcy / Noah Berlatsky, book editor.
    p. cm. -- (Opposing viewpoints)
    Includes bibliographical references and index.
    ISBN 978-0-7377-7244-9 (hardcover) -- ISBN 978-0-7377-7245-6 (pbk.)
 1. Bankruptcy--United States. I. Berlatsky, Noah.
    HG3766.B24 2015
    332.7'50973--dc23

                                                    2014041205

Printed in the United States of America
1 2 3 4 5 6 7 19 18 17 16 15

Contents

Chapter 3: What Are Issues Facing Cities That Declare Bankruptcy?

Chapter 4: When Are Government Bailouts Preferable to Bankruptcy?

Why Consider Opposing Viewpoints?

> "The only way in which a human being can make some approach to knowing the whole of a subject is by hearing what can be said about it by persons of every variety of opinion and studying all modes in which it can be looked at by every character of mind. No wise man ever acquired his wisdom in any mode but this."
>
> *John Stuart Mill*

In our media-intensive culture it is not difficult to find differing opinions. Thousands of newspapers and magazines and dozens of radio and television talk shows resound with differing points of view. The difficulty lies in deciding which opinion to agree with and which "experts" seem the most credible. The more inundated we become with differing opinions and claims, the more essential it is to hone critical reading and thinking skills to evaluate these ideas. Opposing Viewpoints books address this problem directly by presenting stimulating debates that can be used to enhance and teach these skills. The varied opinions contained in each book examine many different aspects of a single issue. While examining these conveniently edited opposing views, readers can develop critical thinking skills such as the ability to compare and contrast authors' credibility, facts, argumentation styles, use of persuasive techniques, and other stylistic tools. In short, the Opposing Viewpoints Series is an ideal way to attain the higher-level thinking and reading skills so essential in a culture of diverse and contradictory opinions.

In addition to providing a tool for critical thinking, Opposing Viewpoints books challenge readers to question their own strongly held opinions and assumptions. Most people form their opinions on the basis of upbringing, peer pressure, and personal, cultural, or professional bias. By reading carefully balanced opposing views, readers must directly confront new ideas as well as the opinions of those with whom they disagree. This is not to argue simplistically that everyone who reads opposing views will—or should—change his or her opinion. Instead, the series enhances readers' understanding of their own views by encouraging confrontation with opposing ideas. Careful examination of others' views can lead to the readers' understanding of the logical inconsistencies in their own opinions, perspective on why they hold an opinion, and the consideration of the possibility that their opinion requires further evaluation.

Evaluating Other Opinions

To ensure that this type of examination occurs, Opposing Viewpoints books present all types of opinions. Prominent spokespeople on different sides of each issue as well as well-known professionals from many disciplines challenge the reader. An additional goal of the series is to provide a forum for other, less known, or even unpopular viewpoints. The opinion of an ordinary person who has had to make the decision to cut off life support from a terminally ill relative, for example, may be just as valuable and provide just as much insight as a medical ethicist's professional opinion. The editors have two additional purposes in including these less known views. One, the editors encourage readers to respect others' opinions—even when not enhanced by professional credibility. It is only by reading or listening to and objectively evaluating others' ideas that one can determine whether they are worthy of consideration. Two, the inclusion of such viewpoints encourages the important critical thinking skill of objectively evaluating an author's credentials and bias. This evaluation will illuminate an author's reasons for taking a particular stance on an issue and will aid in readers' evaluation of the author's ideas.

It is our hope that these books will give readers a deeper understanding of the issues debated and an appreciation of the complexity of even seemingly simple issues when good and honest people disagree. This awareness is particularly important in a democratic society such as ours in which people enter into public debate to determine the common good. Those with whom one disagrees should not be regarded as enemies but rather as people whose views deserve careful examination and may shed light on one's own.

Thomas Jefferson once said that "difference of opinion leads to inquiry, and inquiry to truth." Jefferson, a broadly educated man, argued that "if a nation expects to be ignorant and free . . . it expects what never was and never will be." As individuals and as a nation, it is imperative that we consider the opinions of others and examine them with skill and discernment. The Opposing Viewpoints series is intended to help readers achieve this goal.

David L. Bender and Bruno Leone,
Founders

Introduction

> "Mr. President, I have come to the floor
> today to address this pending legislation.
> This issue should force us to face a fun-
> damental question about who we are as
> a country, how we progress as a society,
> and where our values lie as a people:
> How do we treat our fellow Americans
> who have fallen on hard times, and what
> is our responsibility to cushion those falls
> when they occur?"
>
> —Senator Barack Obama,
> Floor Statement on S.256, the
> Bankruptcy Abuse Prevention and
> Consumer Protection Act of 2005

In 2005 the United States instituted a major bankruptcy reform. Designed to prevent abuse, the law made it more difficult for individuals to clear their debts through bankruptcy.
In particular, the law made it more difficult to file for Chapter
7 bankruptcy, in which debts are discharged completely. Instead, many individuals have to file for Chapter 13, under
which creditors often receive some repayment. In an April 20,
2005, article at CNN, Jeanne Sahadi noted that supporters of
the bill thought it would prevent consumers from using bankruptcy "to clear debts that they can afford to pay." Opponents
of the law, though, argued that it was a giveaway to credit
card companies and put an undue burden on debtors.

Though it was passed almost a decade ago, the bankruptcy
reform law of 2005 continues to be controversial. For instance, Michelle J. White and Wenli Li argue in a December 1,
2009, article on VoxEU.org that the bankruptcy reforms con-
tributed to the 2008 financial crisis and the major recession
that followed. White and Li explain,

In 2005, major reform of US bankruptcy law sharply increased debtors' cost of filing for bankruptcy. This caused a sharp reduction in the number of filings. Because credit card debts and other types of unsecured debt are discharged in bankruptcy, filing for bankruptcy loosens homeowners' budget constraints and makes paying the mortgage easier. Thus the 2005 reform set the stage for an increase in mortgage defaults by making bankruptcy less readily available. We estimate that the reform caused about 800,000 additional mortgage defaults and 250,000 additional foreclosures to occur in each of the past several years—thus contributing to the severity of the financial crisis.

In other words, homeowners had fewer options for debt relief in 2008 than they would have had without bankruptcy reform; as a result, there were more mortgage defaults, more foreclosures, and a worse financial crisis than there would otherwise have been. White and Li recommend reversing the bankruptcy reform to help reduce foreclosures and mortgage defaults.

Donald P. Morgan attempts to assess the success of the bankruptcy reform in a June 4, 2012, post at the website of the Federal Reserve Bank of New York. He points out that the goal of the reform was to reduce the number of bankruptcies filed. Initially, bankruptcies actually accelerated, as debtors hurried to file before the new restrictive laws went into effect. Over the long term, though, Morgan's research suggests that a mild decrease in bankruptcies occurred, and the law could be considered a mild success from that perspective.

Morgan argues that a better judge of success would be whether credit became more readily available. Stricter bankruptcy laws should have lowered the costs of offering credit, since creditors were more likely to be repaid. If costs were lower, credit should be more available. However, Morgan found that credit was not cheaper nor more readily available to consumers. By this measure, then, the bankruptcy reform was not successful.

Mike Konczal is even harsher in his assessment of the bankruptcy reform in a September 15, 2009, article in the *Atlantic*. Konczal argues that the reform had not in fact reduced bankruptcy. Instead, he explains, the main result of the legislation had been to extend the amount of time it takes to file for bankruptcy. "And what happens during that time?" Konczal asks. "The person in question is paying triggered high-interest rates on credit card loans." This is very profitable for credit card companies, and Konczal suggests it may have been the real reason for the legislation from their perspective. "Stringing consumers along for another 2 years+ is a great business improvement, even if it doesn't change a single other thing," he concludes.

One change in the bankruptcy law of 2005 that has turned out to be unexpectedly important is the treatment of student loan debt. Reform in 2005 made it almost impossible in most cases to discharge student loan debt in bankruptcy. There was little discussion of the change prior to passage, according to Tyler Kingkade in an August 15, 2012, article at the *Huffington Post*. However, as tuition costs have increased, student loan debt has become more and more of a burden. Total student debt reached $1 trillion in 2012, outpacing any other kind of consumer debt, including credit cards and car loans. Although some have called to push for changes to bankruptcy to make student loans eligible again, there has been little movement in Congress on the issue.

This volume of *Opposing Viewpoints: Bankruptcy* examines bankruptcy in the current post-2005 reform environment in chapters titled "Is It Wrong to File for Bankruptcy?," "How Should Different Types of Debt Be Dealt with in Bankruptcy?," "What Are Issues Facing Cities That Declare Bankruptcy?," and "When Are Government Bailouts Preferable to Bankruptcy?" The authors debate many of the issues surrounding bankruptcy and discuss weaknesses in the current bankruptcy system and possible future reforms.

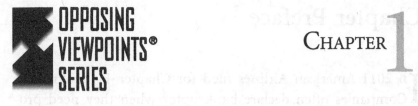

CHAPTER 1

Is It Wrong to File for Bankruptcy?

Chapter Preface

In 2011 American Airlines filed for Chapter 11 bankruptcy. Companies often declare bankruptcy when they need protection for creditors to reorganize the business. However, American Airlines' bankruptcy was unusual in that the chief executive officer of the company, Gerard Arpey, adamantly opposed bankruptcy on moral grounds. Arpey argued that American Airlines had made commitments to its employees, creditors, and stockholders. "I believe it's important to the character of the company and its ultimate long-term success to do your very best to honor those commitments," he was quoted as saying in a November 30, 2011, article by D. Michael Lindsay in the *New York Times*. "It is not good thinking—either at the corporate level or at the personal level—to believe you can simply walk away from your circumstances."

Many people praised Arpey's decision to resign from the company rather than preside over a bankruptcy. He was also lauded for his decision to reject any severance pay. Former senator and president of the University of Oklahoma David Boren said, "This country would be so much better off if we had more people who had Gerard Arpey's sense of responsibility and character as well as ability," as quoted by Terry Maxon in a November 30, 2011, article in the *Dallas Morning News*. Tom Horton, Arpey's replacement, called his predecessor "a man of honor" and praised his "characteristic selflessness," as quoted in a November 29, 2011, article by Ted Reed at TheStreet website.

Some commenters, however, argue that Arpey's moral stance against bankruptcy was misguided. Dan Newman writing at the Motley Fool on February 7, 2012, said that Arpey's refusal to file for bankruptcy did not help the company. Newman explained,

While honesty and moral actions may prove important for a company like Whole Foods, whose brand relies on a certain customer perception, American paid extra labor costs without realizing any benefit from the moral high ground. And even if customers did, for some reason, appreciate American's avoidance of bankruptcy and attempt to honor benefits, the unions did not. Arpey spent five years trying to create new labor agreements without success. Without any new labor agreements, American's labor costs remained 21% higher than Delta's, the largest airline.

Newman concludes that Arpey had not benefited shareholders. By refusing to file bankruptcy in 2003, Arpey simply pushed American Airlines' problems down the road, ending in bankruptcy filing in 2011.

The authors in the following chapter discuss other issues surrounding whether it is right or wrong to file for bankruptcy, focusing on both moral and practical concerns.

> *"When debt becomes more important than people, the system is evil and should be dismantled."*

Bankruptcy Is a Way to Reduce the Immorality of Debt

Charles Hugh Smith

Charles Hugh Smith is the chief writer for the blog Of Two Minds *and a writer for other sites, including the* American Conservative. *In the following viewpoint, he argues that bankruptcy allows debtors to move on with their lives and encourages lenders to lend responsibly. The alternative, he says, is to value the debt more than people, thus putting undue hardship and debt-serfdom on debtors and encouraging financial irresponsibility. He points especially to Greece, which has a massive debt burden and has imposed severe austerity measures to pay for its borrowing. He says the moral thing for Greece to do is repudiate its debts so that it can rebuild and help its people.*

As you read, consider the following questions:

1. Why does Smith argue that lenders should suffer if they extend credit to a poor credit risk?

Charles Hugh Smith, "When Debt Is More Important than People, the System Is Evil," OfTwoMinds.com, February 18, 2012. © 2012 OfTwoMinds.com. All rights reserved. Reproduced by permission.

2. What does Smith say is the acme of debt-serfdom?

3. What does Smith say Greece should do to start disman-
tling the "Empire of Debt"?

*The Empire of Debt has only one end point: a death spiral. It
is evil and must be dismantled.*

Ethics has no place in the Empire of Debt. The financial-
ized status quo is careful to limit the language used to describe the situation in Greece [where the nation is in danger
of default] to the subtexts of "obligations" and "avoiding
chaos."

The Lender Is at Fault

The reality being masked is that debt is now more important
than people. The suffering of the people of Greece is presented as a footnote to the financial play being staged; when
the suffering is noted, it is presented with a peculiar set of un-
spoken subtexts:

1. Looky-loo detachment of the "gosh, look at that wrecked
car, are there any bodies?" sort. People slow down to look at
car crashes, and they revel in videos of riots with the same de-
tached fascination with mayhem that doesn't involve them.
Tsk tsk, how awful, etc.

2. They're reaping what they sowed, "they made their bed,
now they have to sleep in it," i.e., the suffering of Greek non-
elites is the richly deserved consequences of their government
overborrowing.

This begs further investigation. In the normal course of
affairs in corrupt kleptocracies, various elites siphon off most
of the swag and the commoners get just enough shreds to buy
their complicity. In other words, it may well be that the entire
populace of Greece benefitted handsomely from the massive
state borrowing, but it also may well be that the private sector

Greeks received little of the swag. In this case, they don't "deserve" to be forced into debt-serfdom by their Euroland overlords.

The ethics of debt, at least in the officially sanctioned media, boils down to: nobody made them borrow all those euros, and so their suffering is just desserts.

What's lost in this subtext is the responsibility of the lender. Yes, nobody forced Greece to borrow 200 billion euros (or whatever the true total may be), but then nobody forced the lenders to extend the credit in the first place.

Consider an individual who is a visibly poor credit risk. He would like to borrow money to blow on consumption and then stiff the lender, but since he cannot create credit, he has to live within his means.

Now a lender comes along who can create credit out of thin air (via fractional reserve banking) and offers this poor credit risk $100,000 in collateral-free debt at low rates of interest. Who is responsible for the creation and extension of credit? The borrower or the lender? Answer: the lender.

In other words, if the lender is foolish enough to extend huge quantities of credit to a poor credit risk, then it's the lender who should suffer the losses when the borrower defaults.

Debt-Serfdom

This is the basis of bankruptcy laws—or used to be the basis. When an overextended borrower defaults, the debt is cleared, the lender takes the loss/write-down, and the borrower loses whatever collateral was pledged. He is left with the basics to carry on: his auto, clothing, his job, and so on. His credit rating is impaired, and it is now his responsibility to earn back a credible credit rating.

The debt is discharged and the borrower must live within his means without relying on credit. But he is also free of the burdens of servicing the debt.

If the lender is forced into insolvency due to the losses, then so be it: Lenders that cannot differentiate between good and bad credit risks should go under and disappear; that's what happens in a competitive, transparent capitalist economy. Fools who create credit and extend it to poor credit risks must be eliminated from the system as quickly as possible lest they destroy more capital in the future.

The potential for loss and actually bearing the consequences from irresponsible extensions of credit was unacceptable to the banking cartel, so they rewrote the laws. Now student loans in America cannot be discharged in bankruptcy court; they are permanent and must be carried and serviced until death. This is the acme of debt-serfdom.

The global banking cartel has declared Greece's debts to be permanent and its people debt-serfs. More precisely, some privately held debt will be written down, but certainly not all of it, and the debt owed to the European Central Bank cannot be written down a single euro: Greece must pay the interest on the full debt, whatever the costs to its people.

We might ask why the fully-financialized status quo of financial and political elites so carefully insures no shadow of ethics passes over the Greek debt crisis. If they did, it would become obvious that when debt becomes more important than people, the system is evil and should be dismantled.

Yes, evil, as in evil empire: the Empire of Debt that now dominates the global economy is intrinsically evil and cannot be salvaged; the only way to rid the planet of its parasitic, pervasive evil is to dismantle it, all of it, everywhere.

Europe is a good place to start. The only way to dismantle the evil Empire of Debt is to stop obeying its commands: Greece should not pay a single euro on any of its debts, starting with debt owed to the Evil Empire of Debt's favorite tool, the Troika of the EU (European Union), the ECB [European Central Bank] and the IMF [International Monetary Fund].

The Financial Collapse in Greece

The drama had been brewing for the past two years. In the wake of the credit crunch, following the collapse of the American investment bank Lehman Brothers, the financial markets had frozen. There was a sudden and terrifying collapse in world trade: In response, governments everywhere had massively increased their budget deficits in an attempt to steady economies that looked to be on the verge of tipping into a replay of the Great Depression of the 1930s. But as 2009 turned into 2010, and as the fears of another depression eased, the markets started to worry about something else. The cure was starting to look even worse than the disease. And the buildup of sovereign debts, and whether those debts could ever possibly get repaid, was suddenly the issue everyone was worrying about.

There were a dozen different countries the bond dealers could have picked on. But it happened to be Greece.... The country's prime minister, George Papandreou, had been taught a painful lesson in the harsh realities of global finance: When the money runs out, so do your options.... The country's debts were proving quite literally impossible to finance. Already, the Greeks had been forced to appeal for outside help. Now the European Union and the International Monetary Fund had landed in Athens with the promise of a rescue package. But the price they would demand would be a heavy one: cuts on a brutal and massive scale, an end to the easy-money culture that had taken root ..., and a shocking assault on the living standards of ordinary people. That was the price that would have to be paid, and it was no longer negotiable.

Matthew Lynn, Bust: Greece, the Euro and the Sovereign Debt Crisis. *Hoboken, NJ: John Wiley & Sons, 2011, pp. 2–3.*

We are constantly told default and exit from the debtors' prison of the euro would lead to chaos. Unfortunately for the Evil Empire of Debt and its Eurozone army of lackeys, toadies and apparatchiks, this claim is demonstrably false. Thanks to Pater Tenebrarum of the always excellent *Acting Man* financial blog for pointing us to a comprehensive 53-page report from Variant Perception that completely dismantles the fearmongering claims of apocalypse for the Greeks should their government default on its debts.

Default, Not Debt Spiral

The only way forward is default and exit from the debtors' prison of the euro.

Once the debt has been renounced, Greece will have to live within its means, i.e., the goods and services produced by their economy. I think a critically important point has been lost in all the fearmongering: The value of the goods and services produced by an economy remain the same whether they are valued in euros, gold, dollars, bat guano or any other open-market measure of value.

What will impoverish Greece is paying interest on the mountain of debt. If we value total Greek output of goods and services at 100 quatloos, and this economic activity generates a surplus of 10 quatloos, the Greek people can decide to consume that 10 quatloos, invest it or some mix of the two.

If they have to pay 10 quatloos in interest, then there is no capital left to invest in productive assets. As the existing productive assets degrade, wear out and become obsolete, then the goods and services produced will decline, along with the surplus generated. This sets up a positive feedback loop, i.e., a death spiral: as production of value declines, so too does the surplus available to invest in productive assets.

This is why the only way forward is default and exit from the debtors' prison of the euro. The only way forward is to value people more than debt, and to dismantle the evil Empire of Debt.

| "That's 10 years during which you will find it very difficult to get any new credit or at least at decent interest rates."

Bankruptcy Causes Serious Problems and Should Be a Last Resort

Paul Ritz

Paul Ritz is an associate at National Debt Relief, a debt consolidation company. In the following viewpoint, he argues that bankruptcy is not always the best solution for debtors because it does not extinguish all kinds of debts and because it can damage an individual's credit rating. Ritz argues that debt consolidation may be a better option, since it allows individuals to negotiate with creditors without damaging their credit score.

As you read, consider the following questions:

1. According to Ritz, what is the difference between a Chapter 7 and a Chapter 13 bankruptcy?

2. What debts does Ritz say a Chapter 7 bankruptcy will not discharge?

3. In what circumstances does Ritz say a Chapter 7 bankruptcy might be changed to a Chapter 13 bankruptcy?

You say you're so deep in debt that you can't see any way out? You're getting harassing phone calls from debt collectors and credit card companies and are worried that your wages might be garnished? Then you see one of those ads promising to handle your bankruptcy proceeding for less than $500 and ask yourself, why not?

Declaring Bankruptcy

If you do decide this would be your best option, it's important to understand that there are two types—a Chapter 7 and a Chapter 13.

Most people choose a Chapter 7 because it's a way to eliminate certain debts. In comparison, a Chapter 13 is more a way to reorganize and then pay off your debts.

People who choose this type of bankruptcy are required to file a number of documents with the court, including a list of assets and liabilities and current income and liabilities. You'll also be required to go through credit counseling and provide a statement that you did so.

Once you file for a Chapter 7 bankruptcy, you will be assigned a trustee who will oversee your case. He or she will review all of your assets and determine whether they are exempt or nonexempt. In most cases, your assets will all be exempt. This includes items such as equity in your house, equity in your car, your furniture and other such personal possessions. In the event that the trustee determines that you do have nonexempt items, your creditors can file a distribution claim to have them sold so they can be repaid some of what you owe.

A Chapter 7 bankruptcy generally will discharge most of your unsecured debts. This typically includes credit card debts, personal loans, medical bills, past due utility bills, bad checks (unless there was fraud involved), civil court judgments and revolving charge accounts.

Hidden Dangers

Contrary to popular opinion, a Chapter 7 bankruptcy will not eliminate all of your debts. It will not discharge taxes and tax liens, student loan debt, alimony and child support, debts obtained through fraud, condominium or co-op association fees, and several other types such as debts obtained through false pretenses, false representation or fraud.

The second and biggest negative of a Chapter 7 bankruptcy is that it will stay on your credit report for 10 years. That's 10 years during which you will find it very difficult to get any new credit or at least at decent interest rates.

You may find it next to impossible to get a new mortgage or even rent a house or apartment during those years. You will have to give up all your credit cards and you may lose some of your possessions. For example, if you own a boat, a travel trailer or a second home, you can kiss it goodbye, as it will be sold to satisfy some of your debts.

Finally, if you choose a Chapter 7 bankruptcy but the court finds that you have a certain amount of disposable income, it could decide to convert your case into a Chapter 13. This means that instead of being free of most of your debts within 4 to 6 months, you would be required to pay them over a 3- to 5-year period.

Many families let us do debt settlement for them as it will not have as serious an effect on [their] credit as filing for bankruptcy. Our debt counselors can negotiate settlements with your creditors that will save you thousands of dollars and help you become debt free in 24 to 48 months. It's a great solution for people who want to get out of debt but don't want to have a bankruptcy on record.

▌ *"These people need relief now!"*

Bankruptcy Should Be an Emotional and Financial Relief, Not a Traumatic Experience

Joe Fulwiler

Joe Fulwiler is a bankruptcy attorney in Austin, Texas. In the following viewpoint, he argues against Dave Ramsey, a popular financial counselor who warns against bankruptcy. Fulwiler says that many people need bankruptcy and debt relief to get their lives back on track. He points out that living with debt and constant harassment from creditors can be frightening and stressful. He says that bankruptcy does not permanently damage one's credit and that some lenders even seek out people who have recently filed bankruptcy. Fulwiler says that bankruptcy is not the best solution for everyone, but for many it can be a huge relief.

As you read, consider the following questions:

1. What does Fulwiler say is more "gut-wrenching" than bankruptcy?

2. According to Fulwiler, how was Dave Ramsey's bankruptcy different from most people's?

3. How is bankruptcy is supported by Christianity, according to Fulwiler?

If you've found yourself in need of financial help, and have searched the Internet for information on financial matters, you have undoubtedly come across Dave Ramsey's website and his financial management products designed to help people get out of debt and manage their finances. I used to be a big fan of Mr. Ramsey, and most of the information you find on his website is useful. However, his stubborn disdain for bankruptcy is illogical and borders on being deceptive.

Disregard Dave Ramsey

I would like to point out, before I get started on why Dave Ramsey is wrong about bankruptcy, that I am in fact a bankruptcy attorney. I meet with people on a daily basis that have run out of options for paying down their debt. They are often in the process of being sued, or having the family home foreclosed, and they live under daily harassment from creditors. These people need relief now! On the other hand, I also run into people who only have $10,000 of debt, and simply need to manage their finances appropriately to pay down their debts. For those people, bankruptcy may not be the right option. I do not try to sell bankruptcy to people if they don't need it. I merely use the appropriate tool when necessary, and there are some situations where bankruptcy is the right tool.

Here is why I think you should disregard Dave Ramsey's advice on bankruptcy.

1. Dave Ramsey has a specific counseling service that is targeted at people considering bankruptcy. It strikes me as disingenuous to take the position that bankruptcy is never a good option when you are selling a service that competes with bankruptcy. It's hard not to draw the conclusion that he is trying to push his product.

2. He claims that "bankruptcy is a gut-wrenching, life-changing event that causes lifelong damage." It is true that the process of filing bankruptcy can be "gut-wrenching," but when compared to the reality of shouldering a large amount of debt for years to come, it is not as gut-wrenching as being sued, and having the phone ring for months, day in and day out, from creditors calling to collect unpaid debts. I've seen many people struggle to make interest payments on an enormous amount of debt for years, only to reach retirement age and realize they are out of time and penniless, and they are then forced to file bankruptcy anyway. That's gut-wrenching! If they had just admitted to themselves earlier that they needed a fresh start, they could have been saving for retirement instead of paying interest on a debt that they really had no hope of repaying.

Everyone Is Not Dave Ramsey

3. Dave Ramsey uses his own personal experience of bankruptcy to support his claims of detrimental emotional effects caused by bankruptcy. However, Dave Ramsey's bankruptcy experience is very out of the ordinary.

1. Dave Ramsey was an overleveraged real estate speculator that couldn't liquidate his assets fast enough when the bank called his loans, leaving him with millions of dollars of debt. Most people who face the possibility of filing for bankruptcy are not overleveraged real estate speculators, but rather are normal families with both parents working to keep food on the table and pay the bills. They might have experienced an income reduction due to the loss of a job, the loss of a spouse's ability to work, or another life-changing event such as divorce.

2. Dave Ramsey waited years before filing for bankruptcy. He allowed himself to be sued, harassed, and frustrated. If Dave Ramsey had realized the state of his financial situation sooner, and realized that bankruptcy is not a defeat, but a tool created to help people, he could have avoided the anguish he endured.

3. If Dave Ramsey had not filed for bankruptcy, it is very unlikely that he would have enjoyed the success that he has today. It was because he filed bankruptcy that he was able to move past his debt and begin his new life debt free.

4. *One reason Dave Ramsey has become so successful is that he has explored the spiritual component of debt* that people experience. This experience is oftentimes very dark and humbling and can cause emotional distress. And it is precisely because the experience of being a debtor is so dark and serious that I believe that bankruptcy relief is essential for many people. Dave Ramsey encourages people in a spiritual way and helps them get through their dark hours, and they need that. However, it strikes me as abusive to prey on people's religious beliefs and feelings of guilt to guide them away from a fresh start in bankruptcy. "Pay your debts" is generally good advice, but not for those at rock bottom who have no ability to repay. If it becomes clear that they can't pay their debts, you have to give them a way out that is achievable, reasonable, prompt, and realistic. They need relief. They have already been struggling for so long. When I meet with potential clients about bankruptcy, the topic of suicidal thoughts comes up surprisingly often. Getting them relief and a fresh start can literally be a life or death issue. Divorce also comes up a lot. Getting a debtor relief can also save his or her marriage. This is serious stuff, with deep spiritual implications.

The Bible and Debt

5. *Using Christianity to lead people away from bankruptcy is ironic,* because forgiving debts every 7 years comes straight

Dave Ramsey's Advice

By the time [Dave] Ramsey was 26, he has written, he had become a real estate millionaire, but the leverage inherent in the business caught up with him. Ultimately, Ramsey has said, he had to declare bankruptcy.

Ramsey ... attaches a simple lesson to this: Debt is corrosive, almost to the point of being a moral failure. "The borrower is slave to the lender," Ramsey says, invoking Proverbs.

Ramsey is overtly religious, and his for-profit Financial Peace University is billed as "a biblically based curriculum that teaches people how to handle money God's ways."

Ramsey, 53, got his start in radio with a show in Nashville in 1992. By the time he came to the attention of the coastal elites in the mid-2000s, his show was already a national force, with 2 million listeners. Ramsey tells people that no matter the state of their financial lives, there is hope for recovery if they will just take responsibility and start to take action.

Felix Salmon with Susie Poppick, "Save Like Dave Ramsey ... Just Don't Invest Like Him," Money, September 26, 2013.

from the Bible. Deuteronomy 15:1 says "at the end of every seven years, you must cancel debts." This passage was the basis for the practice of debtor's relief in the ecclesiastical courts of old, which evolved into courts of equity, which were a forebear of modern U.S. bankruptcy courts. In my bankruptcy law practice, it has been striking to me how many of the judges, trustees, and attorneys in the bankruptcy legal field are deeply spiritual people. (Note: Our bankruptcy law says that if you get a bankruptcy discharge, you can't file bankruptcy again for

8 years. Until the bankruptcy law changed in 2005, the rule was that you couldn't file bankruptcy again for 7 years. If you trace the origin of that 7-year rule, it goes all the way back to Deuteronomy.)

6. *It is immoral to borrow if you know you are not going to repay, and it's also immoral to not repay your debts if you have the money to do so.* But it's not immoral to not pay if you can't pay. If you borrowed in good faith, with an honest intent to repay, and your plans simply didn't work out, and you just can't repay your debts, there is nothing morally wrong with that. Acknowledging facts is moral. Coming to terms with the truth (such as "I am never going to be able to pay off this debt") is a good thing to do.

It Will Not Harm Your Credit

7. *Dave Ramsey also argues that bankruptcy will harm your credit.* That's hogwash for many reasons.

- If you are a good candidate for bankruptcy, your credit is already ruined.

- Also, filing bankruptcy helps your credit recover more quickly because it discharges your debt, thus giving you a better ability to repay any new, post-bankruptcy debt. Creditors like that. Many of my bankruptcy clients have been former realtors, mortgage brokers, and auto sales-men who have been in the business of trying to get people approved for loans. They consistently tell me that it is much easier to get someone approved for a loan if they filed bankruptcy and waited 2–3 years than if they didn't file bankruptcy and still have all that old debt and all those late pays on their credit report.

- Also, you can only file bankruptcy every 8 years, so if you have recently filed bankruptcy, any new lender doesn't have to worry about you running out and filing bankruptcy. This is another reason why some lenders SEEK OUT people who have just filed bankruptcy.

- Also, as Dave Ramsey states so clearly in his books, you are probably better off never borrowing again. So who cares what your credit score is?

8. *It is true that the fact that you filed bankruptcy will be on your credit report for 10 years,* but most lenders don't give much weight to events older than 2–3 years. They know that many people hit bumps in the road and then get their financial lives back on track.

> *"You are 25, give or take. You lived and you learned. You should not have to be at a disadvantage because of your 'free-Slinky' credit card."*

Filing for Bankruptcy in Your Twenties May Improve Your Finances

Leonora Gorelik

Leonora Gorelik is an attorney in Southern California. In the following viewpoint, she argues that filing for bankruptcy can be a good decision for those in their twenties and thirties. She says that filing for bankruptcy can help young people start saving for retirement and can get their finances in order before they marry. She says it is also a good way to move forward and that it can help make sure individuals can pay student loans, which cannot be discharged through bankruptcy, by eliminating other debts.

As you read, consider the following questions:

1. Why does Gorelik say individuals may qualify for Chapter 7 bankruptcy before marriage but not after?

2. What does Gorelik suggest may happen to Social Security before retirement?

3. Which does Gorelik say individuals should pay first, student loans or credit cards, and why?

Reason 1—You Will Probably Be Getting Married Soon and Merging Your Finances

You are probably going to get married. And with that comes the oh-so-fun merging of the finances. I can assure you that it is a lot better to be the person saying, "yeah, once upon a time I filed for bankruptcy. I learned a lot. I don't have any debt now, other than my student loans, and I have managed to save for retirement and put money away for a rainy day since that time. Oh, and because it was a while ago, my credit is pretty great." You don't want to be the person saying, "So I have some debt. It's totally my fault. I was stupid in college. I am working hard to pay it off. I am not putting any money away in savings and a large portion of my check will have to go towards the credit cards. Yeah, I won't be able to contribute to the house saving budget for a long time. I could have filed for bankruptcy, but it's against my beliefs. I want to pay it off." I think you can guess what your spouse-to-be would rather hear from you. Additionally, while you may qualify for Chapter 7 (the simpler of the bankruptcies) now, you may not qualify once you are married, because of the additional household income. Why wait?

Retirement

Reason 2—You Should Be Paying Yourself (Like the Rich People)

You are 25 or so. You should be putting money towards retirement. Listening to the news and Suze Orman [a television host and financial advisor], you know that Social Security may not be there for you and even if it is, it likely won't be enough. Starting to put money away when you are in your 20s, versus when you are in your 30s, makes a big difference. . . . Even if you are paying $150/mo. (and my guess is it's

Student Loan Debt

The halcyon days of higher education in the early 1970s, when the typical high school graduate could put him- or herself through college for a few thousand dollars (at most) in student loan debt and be able to repay this debt by working over the summers, are long gone. Today, about two-thirds of college students require loans to make it through, and the typical undergraduate borrower leaves school with more than twenty thousand dollars in student loan debt. For graduate students, that amount more than doubles, to forty-two thousand dollars. Tuition inflation has outpaced the consumer price index (CPI) during this time period by a factor of about two to one.

Also during this period, the Higher Education Act was amended six times, becoming progressively more lucrative for the lenders and less beneficial for the students. Over time, legislators gave more support to the interests of the student loan companies and the federal government than to the interests of the students. Bankruptcy protections, statutes of limitations, refinancing rights, and many other standard consumer protections vanished for student loans—and only for student loans. Concurrently, draconian collection tools were legislated into existence, and they provided unprecedented and unrivaled collection powers to the loan industry, including giving it the ability to garnishee a borrower's wages, tax returns, Social Security, and disability income—all without a court order. Today, the student loan is an inescapable and profitable debt instrument unlike any other.

Alan Michael Collinge, The Student Loan Scam: The Most Oppressive Debt in U.S. History—and How We Can Fight Back. *Boston, MA: Beacon Press, 2009, pp. 4–5.*

a lot more), this is money you are not putting into savings and retirement. Even the *Rich Dad, Poor Dad* guy [financial advisor Robert Kiyosaki] says that you should pay yourself first. Struggling to pay off your credit cards is not paying yourself first. Oh yeah, and that guy's company filed for bankruptcy and he is doing great financially, so bankruptcy is not just for the poor folks and by no means makes you a failure, it makes you pragmatic.

Reason 3—You Lived and You Learned and Now You Want to Move On

You are 25, give or take. You lived and you learned. You should not have to be at a disadvantage because of your "free-Slinky" credit card [some companies gave out toys, like Slinkies, with new credit cards to college students]. If you don't know what I am referring to, then they probably stopped giving out free Slinkies as a reward for you opening a new credit card when you are in college. Guess what, everyone likes a free Slinky. I got a free Slinky. I was still trying to pay for that Slinky after graduating law school. You live and you learn. If you have a bunch of debts you've been making no headway on, it's time to do something about them. There is no reason why you should have to struggle, not feel safe, not be able to afford health insurance and other basics that you should have, because you made mistakes while walking back to your dorm from class, 8 years ago! It's time to just admit that it was stupid, but also to just be, here it goes again, pragmatic. You are an adult. You want to start making smart financial decisions, rather than still paying off the Slinky. You want to save and you don't want a large chunk of your paycheck going toward those credit cards.

Student Loans

Reason 4—You Have Student Loans

You don't want to get behind on your student loans. You know that saying that there will always be "death and taxes," well they should add "student loans" to that. In fact, sometimes older taxes can be discharged in bankruptcy, not so much the student loans. Yes, there are options, but getting behind on your student loans is not good. You should avoid it. You should certainly not be repaying your credit card debt, if it's making affording your student loans difficult and/or impossible. Trust me on this and anyone who tells you otherwise is wrong, plain and simple.

Finally, this [viewpoint] is obviously on the lighter side and I am not proposing that you take the decision to file for bankruptcy lightly, but I am saying it may improve your life and turn out to be a very smart financial move that makes your life easier, and ultimately better and more productive. . . .

Periodical and Internet Sources Bibliography

The following articles have been selected to supplement the diverse views presented in this chapter.

Danny Fisher	"How I Emerged from Bankruptcy to Grow a Thriving Company," *CNN Money*, January 20, 2014.
Trent Hamm	"Personal Finance Lessons from the Detroit Bankruptcy," *Christian Science Monitor*, July 26, 2013.
Susan Johnston	"5 Bankruptcy Myths Debunked," *U.S. News & World Report*, May 14, 2012.
Parija Kavilanz	"Doctors Driven to Bankruptcy," *CNN*, April 8, 2013.
Lynnette Khalfani-Cox	"The Different Degrees of Bankruptcy, Explained," *Ebony*, June 19, 2014.
John Morgan	"MarketWatch: Bankruptcies May Be Helping America Grow," *Newsmax*, February 8, 2013.
Marie Paseková	"Personal Bankruptcy and Its Social Implications," *International Advances in Economic Research*, August 2013.
Steve Rhode	"Bankruptcy Should Be the Last Resort, Many Say, but That's Just Not True," *Huffington Post*, August 3, 2012.
Gene Sollows	"The Morality of Bankruptcy," *Bankruptcy Blog* (Bailey and Galyen Law Firm), August 3, 2012.
John Skiba	"Is It Immoral to File Bankruptcy?," Skiba Law Group, August 15, 2012.
Liz Skinner	"Coming Back from Bankruptcy," *Investment-News*, June 2, 2014.

OPPOSING
VIEWPOINTS®
SERIES

CHAPTER 2

How Should Different Types of Debt Be Dealt with in Bankruptcy?

Chapter Preface

One of the biggest reasons people file Chapter 7 bankruptcy is because of credit card debt. In most cases, credit card debt can be discharged through bankruptcy, meaning that once bankruptcy is completed, the credit card debt is wiped out.

An individual may not be able to wipe out credit card debt if the credit card company can prove that the debt was incurred through fraud. Basically, if a person used a card to incur a debt without ever intending to pay it back, the debt may not be dischargeable. For example, if an individual spends more than $650 on luxury goods using a single credit card within ninety days of filing for bankruptcy, the credit card company can argue that the person filing for bankruptcy was never intending to pay for those goods. In that case, the debts incurred will not be discharged in bankruptcy, according to attorney Bret A. Maidman in the article "Credit Card Debt in Chapter 7 Bankruptcy" on Nolo.com. The credit card company must specifically dispute charges with the bankruptcy court to prevent discharge, but if the company successfully proves that an individual committed fraud, that person might have to pay the charges and could even face criminal prosecution.

An article at Lawyers.com titled "Credit Card Debt in Chapter 7 Bankruptcy" advises those filing for bankruptcy that to avoid possible disputes with the credit card company, they should "stop using [their] credit cards right now if [they're] seriously considering bankruptcy." The article also recommends that individuals filing for bankruptcy should inform their attorneys if they had used a credit card in the past few months before the bankruptcy filing. The article also says that it is important for individuals filing for bankruptcy to collect pay stubs and financial statements so that they can show they did not commit fraud in filing for a credit card. Finally, the article notes that in some cases, if a debtor has large amounts of questionable credit card debt, it might be better to file Chapter 13 rather than Chapter 7 bankruptcy. Debtors may have to pay back some of the debt, but there is a better chance of being able to discharge some, or most, of the debt.

The following chapter examines resolving several types of debt through bankruptcy, including student loans, medical debts, and mortgages.

> "Under the current system, it is all but impossible to get student loans wiped out through bankruptcy, unlike most other forms of unsecured debt such as credit card and medical bills."

Congress Needs to Change Bankruptcy Laws to Apply to Student Loans

Devon Merling

Devon Merling is an attorney and a journalist who has written for the Deseret News, *a daily newspaper in Salt Lake City, Utah. In the following viewpoint, she argues that student debt is skyrocketing, which hurts both students and the country, since students with debt cannot get back on their feet and participate fully in the economy. She argues that one important solution to the problem would be to allow student loans to be discharged in bankruptcy so that those who cannot repay can wipe out their debts. She concludes that even changes to bankruptcy laws cannot entirely fix the student debt problem and that other alterations to the laws are needed.*

As you read, consider the following questions:

1. According to the viewpoint, what is Obama's plan to deal with student loan debt?

2. How do young Americans' unemployment rates compare with unemployment rates overall, as told by Merling?

3. What would be the terms of the "qualified loans" for students that Merling discusses?

This week [in August 2013], President Barack Obama introduced a proposal that would give colleges federal money based on performance and affordability for students. Such measures, Obama said, would require accountability at institutes of higher education across the country in an effort to curb the escalating costs of student loans.

Experts say there may be an additional way to solve the student debt crisis: bankruptcy law.

Under the current system, it is all but impossible to get student loans wiped out through bankruptcy, unlike most other forms of unsecured debt such as credit card and medical bills. And legal experts say this is creating a generation of Americans who are unable to get out from under the crushing weight of college debt.

"If borrowers don't have the money, they're not paying anyway," said Daniel Austin, a bankruptcy law professor at Northeastern University. "But because they can't get loans discharged, they can't participate in the credit economy. They're off the economic grid. They're the indentured generation."

The Student Loan Burden

A substantial chunk of student loan debt has been a growing fact of life for many Americans. The Consumer Financial Protection Bureau [CFPB] found that total student loan debt is approaching $1.2 trillion, which would exceed credit card debt by more than 28 percent, using Federal Reserve data. Forty-five percent of all American families now have student loans, according to a report released this week by David Bergeron and Joe Valenti from the Center for American Progress, a progressive think tank. And the average student loan balance for a 25-year-old has jumped 91 percent from 2003 to 2012, from $10,649 to $20,326, a recent study from the Federal Reserve Bank of New York showed.

With unemployment high, particularly among young Americans—12.6 percent for 20- to 24-year-olds compared with the overall rate of 7.4 percent, according to July's jobs report—default rates on student loans are on the rise as well. According to a New York Federal Reserve study, in 2011, 14.4 percent, or 5.4 million of the 37 million borrowers who had outstanding student loans, had at least one past due payment. That number is more than 7 million borrowers this year, according to the CFPB. And the 2013 New York Federal Reserve study showed the proliferation of student loans means that students are delaying other major life purchases like homes and cars and even delaying life milestones like marriage and having children.

"There's this [idea] that if you go to college, then you're able to get a job, and you're on your way in life," Austin said. "But education has become so expensive . . . and people are coming out of college with $50,000 to $100,000 in debt. Then they meet hard times and now they become this permanent underclass. It's horrible. We ought not be doing that in this country."

"They're in a different economy than we are," he said. "If we at least allow them to discharge that debt in bankruptcy, they can return to be participants in the economy."

The Muddled Mess of Bankruptcy Law

Although bankruptcy reform legislation passed in 2005 placed a number of hurdles on the ability of people to file for bank-

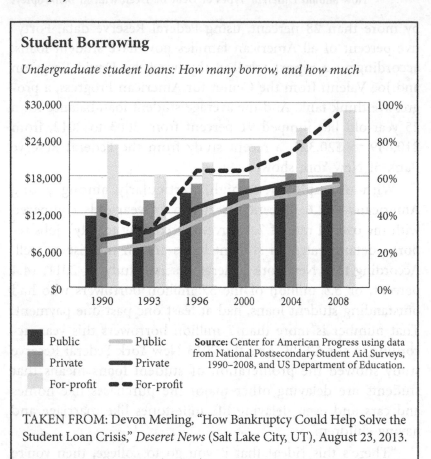

Student Borrowing

Undergraduate student loans: How many borrow, and how much

Legend:
- Public (bar)
- Private (bar)
- For-profit (bar)
- Public (line)
- Private (line)
- For-profit (line)

Source: Center for American Progress using data from National Postsecondary Student Aid Surveys, 1990–2008, and US Department of Education.

TAKEN FROM: Devon Merling, "How Bankruptcy Could Help Solve the Student Loan Crisis," *Deseret News* (Salt Lake City, UT), August 23, 2013.

ruptcy, the number of filings jumped when the recession hit, according to the *Wall Street Journal*. While the number has decreased from the 2011 high of 1.53 million, slightly more than 1 million Americans filed for protection last year, according to Bergeron and Valenti. In bankruptcy, a borrower can wipe out most of his unsecured debt entirely, or repay a portion of it over three to five years. This gives what bankruptcy practitioners and courts have called a "fresh start." But the ability to discharge student loans in bankruptcy has been eroded over the years to the point where now the borrower has to prove that any student loan, even a privately issued one, would cause an "undue hardship" to them in order to get it discharged. Whether a debtor can prove this or not may depend completely on which state the debtor lives in, as the Supreme Court has not provided guidance on what the standard means, and courts interpret it in different ways, according to Austin.

Another wrinkle is that in order to discharge a student loan debt, a debtor needs to file a separate action and argue in front of the bankruptcy court, a process that usually requires an attorney and money. And according to an April report from the National Consumer Law Center, a legal services non-profit agency for low-income consumers, most individual debtors, especially those most in need of a hardship discharge, are not able to afford the costs needed to go to court.

"The reason we have bankruptcy laws is that going back to the founding of this country, we believe people get a second chance," said Bergeron, one of the authors of the Center for American Progress report. "Even for federal loans, if you as a student go into programs that don't adequately prepare you for the work force, that is, if you're prepared in college but can't find a job in your field, through no fault of your own, you shouldn't have the obligation of repaying that loan. That creates some fundamental unfairness that is inconsistent with reasons for the bankruptcy system."

Reforming the Code

Experts have proposed a number of fixes that would help out borrowers stuck under unmanageable debt burdens.

Austin has proposed allowing all private loans to be dischargeable, as he believes lenders should not get the "best of both worlds": lending to whomever they want at whatever terms they want while not having to participate in the loan forgiveness programs—in which a borrower repays an affordable amount over 20–25 years before getting the rest discharged—required of government-backed loans. He also proposed allowing bankruptcy courts to value a debtor's student loan at its fair market value, which is what another investor would be willing to pay to buy the loan off the original lender, and discharge anything above that value. A similar process is currently available to some debtors on their mortgages in bankruptcy.

Bergeron and Valenti propose creating a set of "qualified loans" that meet certain lending standards: reasonable interest rates and fees, deferment and forbearance provisions similar to today's federal student loans, and access to income-based repayment. Loans that shared these characteristics would be unlikely to substantially harm debtors, and so would remain non-dischargeable in bankruptcy. But loans that did not meet these standards, whether public or private, would be dischargeable.

But given the enormity of the student loan problem, even experts who propose bankruptcy reform think other issues must be addressed to control costs and make student loans a good bargain for young borrowers.

"Bankruptcy doesn't solve the whole problem," Austin said. "Thirty million households owe student debt. There are different figures on default, but the overall average may be 30 percent [of student loan borrowers] depending on what set of numbers you look at. That's a lot of people, and [it] might be better if we have them back in the economic grid."

Bergeron thinks that it's going to take a lot more than even the president's proposal and bankruptcy to fix the system. He proposes looking at institutions, both for profit and nonprofit, who are doing innovative things to get students to graduation and employment. "It's gonna take more than those two pieces—it takes more than the president's plan and bankruptcy reform. It really needs to be everyone thinking about driving down costs and improving quality. Because if we don't do it, somebody else will. And by somebody else I mean some other country will. And they're going to kill us."

"*Just the possibility of obtaining a settlement should encourage needy borrowers to move forward with an adversary proceeding.*"

Bankruptcy May Discharge Student Loans in Some Cases

Isaac Bowers

Isaac Bowers is a senior program manager in the communications and outreach unit of Equal Justice Works; he is responsible for the organization's educational debt relief initiatives. In the following viewpoint, he reports on the case of Michael Hedlund, a law school graduate who sued to have his student loan debt discharged. Though the procedure is more difficult and more costly than the normal bankruptcy process, Bowers says, Hedlund did succeed after ten years of litigation in proving that his student loans were an undue hardship, and he succeeded in getting some of the loans discharged. Bowers says this suggests that more borrowers should go to court to get their student loan debt reduced or discharged.

As you read, consider the following questions:

1. How much did Hedlund borrow for law school, and what circumstances made it impossible for him to pay back his loans, according to Bowers?

2. What is the Brunner standard, according to the viewpoint?

3. What does the study by Jason Iuliano suggest about those who have student loan debt?

A 10-year court battle waged by Michael Hedlund, a graduate of Willamette [University] law school, to discharge his student loans has recently ended with a 9th U.S. Circuit Court of Appeals decision partially discharging his loans.

Undue Hardship

Hedlund borrowed about $85,000 to get his undergraduate and law degrees, then failed the bar exam three times. He ultimately took a job as a juvenile counselor. At 33, married and with a child, he declared bankruptcy. His case has potentially large implications for borrowers.

It's pretty well known by now that student loans cannot be discharged through the normal bankruptcy process.

Instead, Congress requires student loan borrowers to initiate an adversary proceeding, a separate lawsuit filed within the bankruptcy case, in which they have to prove that repaying their student loan debt would be an "undue hardship."

In the absence of any further guidance from Congress on what constitutes an undue hardship, most courts now apply what is called the "Brunner standard."

That standard requires a borrower to prove three things: One, that the borrower and any dependents cannot maintain a minimal standard of living based on current income and expenses; two, that additional circumstances indicate this is

A Debt Discharged

A Buffalo bankruptcy judge discharged $56,299 debt of a 64-year-old who borrowed $16,900 for an education that was never completed. The judge found that the unusual facts warranted a discharge under 11 USC § 523(a)(8)(B). The debtor asserted that she had just been laid off from her $11-an-hour assembly line job, had no prospects of additional income, and had used her savings to help support her aging parents. In such circumstances, the Second Circuit applies a three-part test under *Brunner* [referring to *Marie Brunner v. New York State Higher Education Services Corp.*]; would repayment prevent the debtor from sustaining a minimal standard of living? Is the debtor's position unlikely to improve in the future? Did the debtor make good-faith efforts to satisfy the debt? The court agreed with the debtor's factual assertions, finding that the debtor had an $11/hr assembly line job and recently was laid off. She had no prospects of additional income and had used the only large sum she ever had to support her aging parents. According to the court, this satisfied *Brunner*.

Dana Shilling, *Lawyer's Desk Book*, 2014 Edition. *New York: Wolters Kluwer Law & Business, 2014.*

likely to be the case for a significant portion of the borrower's repayment period; and three, that the borrower made a good faith effort to repay the loans.

Some Bad News

The conventional wisdom is that the need for a separate proceeding—for which many bankrupt borrowers will be unable to afford a lawyer—and the stringency with which courts apply this standard make it virtually impossible for borrowers to discharge their student loans. And, in some respects, Hedlund's case confirms this.

Hedlund was represented pro bono by Morrison and Foerster, one of the top bankruptcy firms in the country, which is unlikely to be an option for most borrowers. And, of course, Hedlund was a law school graduate himself.

It's also notable that, due in part to some unusual circumstances such as a judge passing away, it took Hedlund nearly 10 years to earn the partial discharge. Many borrowers will not want to persist through litigation nearly that lengthy.

On the other hand, Hedlund settled with one of the holders of his student loans shortly after filing his adversary proceeding. Just the possibility of obtaining a settlement should encourage needy borrowers to move forward with an adversary proceeding.

Some Relief

As important for future plaintiffs, the 9th Circuit Court also upheld the bankruptcy court's relatively reasonable application of the facts in Hedlund's case to the Brunner standard.

For example, the 9th Circuit Court agreed there was considerable evidence the family's expenses, including two cell phones for the family and leasing a reliable car, could be seen as reasonable and that the excess expenses—including cable and children's haircuts—could be deemed marginal.

The bankruptcy court had also rejected arguments that Hedlund should find another part-time job while noting that his wife could be expected to work three days a week rather than one. The 9th Circuit Court agreed with this analysis as well, holding there was considerable evidence Hedlund had maximized his income and declining to attribute his wife's underemployment to bad faith. These parameters provide hope—and, more importantly, good precedent—for future plaintiffs who want to earn discharges without suffering complete material deprivation or working abnormally long hours.

The 9th Circuit Court also upheld relatively reasonable parameters regarding the effort Hedlund had to make to repay his loans. For example, it agreed with the bankruptcy court that Hedlund was justified in rejecting repayment options offered by his loan servicer that would have entailed monthly payments he could not have afforded and that would still have meant repaying his loans for thirty years.

Overall, Hedlund's case is hopeful precedent. Borrowers should also be aware of a study by Jason Iuliano which suggests that in 2007 alone, there were 69,000 borrowers who were good candidates for relief but fewer than 300 actually attempted to discharge their loans. Iuliano's study also finds evidence that plaintiffs filing adversary proceedings on their own are as likely to prevail as those with attorneys.

The Student Loan Ranger continues to lobby for legislation such as the Private [Student] Loan Bankruptcy Fairness Act of 2013 and the Fairness for Struggling Students Act of 2013 that will restore fairness to the bankruptcy code for private student loan borrowers and to advocate for legislation that will reinstate bankruptcy protections for federal student loan borrowers. In the meantime, Hedlund's experience and Iuliano's study argue that more borrowers in bankruptcy should assert their rights under the undue hardship standard—even if they have to represent themselves.

> "Under current law, home mortgages are treated differently than any other type of debt. Bankruptcy judges are prohibited from altering the terms of a mortgage in any way."

Judges Should Be Allowed to Reorganize Mortgages in Bankruptcy

Dean Baker

Dean Baker is a macroeconomist and codirector of the Center for Economic and Policy Research in Washington, DC. In the following viewpoint, he argues that homeowners are being crushed by the financial crisis and that they need relief from underwater mortgages in which the value of the house is less than the remaining payment on the mortgage. He points out that Congress should allow judges to reorganize mortgages in bankruptcy proceedings, as this would substantially help financially troubled homeowners. Short of that, Baker suggests that governments can use their eminent domain power to seize property to condemn underwater mortgages.

As you read, consider the following questions:

1. What does Baker say progressive members of Congress debated in the fall of 2008?

2. According to Baker, what was San Bernardino's relationship with the housing bubble?

3. Why does Baker argue that Mortgage Resolution Partners (MRP) should be able to make money from condemning underwater mortgages?

Ever since the housing bubble collapsed, the federal government has refused to take major initiatives to help underwater homeowners [those mortgages that are more expensive than the value of the homes]. As a result, we are likely to see close to 1 million foreclosures both this year [2012] and next, with the numbers only gradually slipping back to normal levels by the end of the decade.

Mortgage Relief Is Needed

The inaction cannot be attributed to a lack of opportunity. At the time the Troubled Asset Relief Program (TARP) bailout was being debated in the fall of 2008, many progressive members of Congress wanted to have a provision that would at least temporarily alter bankruptcy law to allow judges to rewrite the terms of a mortgage.

Under current law, home mortgages are treated differently than any other type of debt. Bankruptcy judges are prohibited from altering the terms of a mortgage in any way. If a homeowner cannot meet the terms of the mortgage, they lose the house. Congress could have allowed bankruptcy judges to rewrite mortgages that were written during the housing bubble frenzy, but it backed away from this opportunity.

Similarly, Congress could have temporarily changed the rules on foreclosure to allow foreclosed homeowners to stay in their homes for a substantial period of time (for example, five

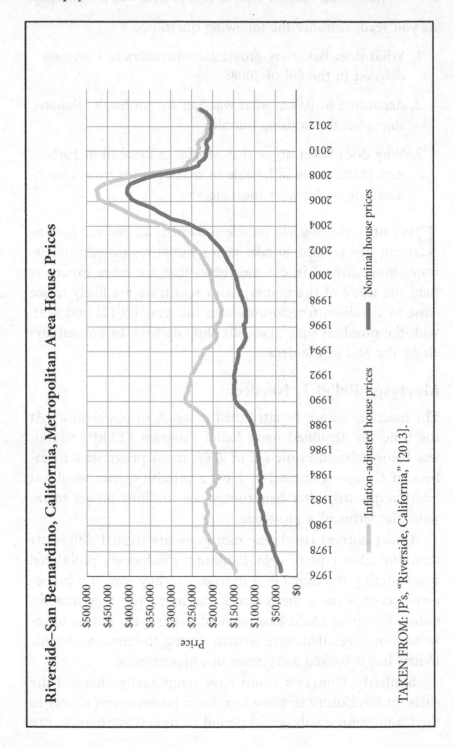

Riverside–San Bernardino, California, Metropolitan Area House Prices

TAKEN FROM: JP's, "Riverside, California," [2013].

years) as renters paying the market rent. This would have assured underwater homeowners substantial housing security.

Either of these measures would have radically altered the relationship between investors and homeowners. They would have given homeowners a serious weapon that they could have used to threaten lenders and hopefully persuade them to agree to modify underwater mortgages. However, since Congress did not take any action to shore up the position of homeowners, we are still sitting here with more than 11 million homeowners underwater, five years after house prices began their plunge.

This failure at the national level provides the backdrop for a plan by a group of investors, Mortgage Resolution Partners (MRP), to try to get through some of the morass in the housing market. MRP has been working with public officials in San Bernardino, California, to arrange to use the government's power of eminent domain [to seize property] to condemn underwater mortgages.

Ground Zero

As background, San Bernardino is ground zero in the housing bubble [referring to an economic bubble that affected the US housing market in several states, where housing prices peaked in early 2006 and reached record lows in 2012]. Prices doubled or even tripled in the bubble years. They plunged when the bubble burst, with prices now often less than half of their 2006 peaks. Half of the mortgages in the county are underwater.

This collapse has not only destroyed the life savings of hundreds of thousands of homeowners, it also has wrecked the economy of the region. In this context, the prospect of using the power to condemn property to bring many underwater homeowners back above water must sound very appealing.

MRP's plan is to have the county condemn underwater mortgages in private mortgage pools. The logic is that these underwater mortgages are causing serious harm to the community. When people are seriously underwater in their homes, they are likely to lack both the means and the incentive to properly maintain their homes. Of course, the monthly payment on a mortgage that might exceed the current value of a home by 50 percent or more (and carry a high interest rate) is a huge drain on the purchasing power of homeowners.

The case for focusing on mortgages in private mortgage pools is that it is generally quite difficult to sell these mortgages out of the pool. This means that even if, in principle, it might be advantageous for both the investors and the homeowners to have pools sell underwater mortgages to third parties like MRP who would rewrite the terms, the rules of the mortgage pools make it unlikely that the mortgage will be sold.

This is exactly the sort of situation where public action like condemnation is appropriate. The public action allows for a solution that can benefit all the parties but is obstructed by bureaucratic rules that were written to cover a different set of circumstances. (It is important to remember that investors can contest in court the compensation they are provided for condemned mortgages to ensure that they get fair market value.)

A Step Forward

It is difficult to see a good argument against this approach. Some have claimed that this sort of tactic will cause lenders to be more reluctant to lend in the future. If the point is that lenders may have second thoughts the next time house prices go into a bubble, then we should certainly hope that condemnation will have this effect.

Others have been critical because MRP is a private company that is doing this to make a profit. I've met with several of the top people at MRP; they certainly don't hide the fact that they expect to make money on this deal. But that hardly seems a reason for nixing the plan. There are very few instances where there has been a public condemnation in which private firms didn't stand to profit in some way.

MRP's plan is not going to rescue the country's underwater homeowners. At best, it will directly help the limited segment of this group whose mortgages are in private-label securities. However, it may serve as an example of the benefits of principal write-downs, and perhaps prod Fannie and Freddie [referring to the Federal National Mortgage Association, commonly known as Fannie Mae, and the Federal Home Loan Mortgage Corporation, known as Freddie Mac], as well as the banks, to be more willing to go this route.

> *"Allowing mortgage modification in bankruptcy also could unleash a torrent of bankruptcies."*

Judges Should Not Be Allowed to Reorganize Mortgages in Bankruptcy

Todd J. Zywicki

Todd J. Zywicki is a law professor at George Mason University. In the following viewpoint, he argues that allowing judges to rewrite the terms of mortgages would cause numerous problems. He says it would increase new mortgage prices and would flood and overwhelm bankruptcy courts, as borrowers would try to get their mortgages restructured. He also argues that having judges rewrite mortgages would damage the entire credit market, leading to harm of the economy.

As you read, consider the following questions:

1. Why does Zywicki believe mortgage costs would rise if judges could reorganize mortgages?

2. What situation does Zywicki describe to show how judges reorganizing bankruptcy could result in abuse?

3. Why does Zywicki say Congress should not deal with the rising number of foreclosures through bankruptcy, and what does he suggest Congress should do instead?

The nation faces a foreclosure crisis of historic proportions, and there is an understandable desire on the part of the federal government to "do something" to help. House Judiciary [Committee] chairman John Conyers' bill, which is moving swiftly through Congress (and companion legislation introduced by Sen. Richard Durbin) would allow bankruptcy judges to modify home mortgages by reducing both the interest rate and principal amount on the loan. This would be a profound mistake.

More Expensive Mortgages

Mortgage modification would indeed provide a windfall for some troubled homeowners—but its costs will be borne by aspiring future homeowners, and by any American who uses credit of any kind, from car loans to credit cards. The ripple effects could further roil America's consumer credit markets.

In the first place, mortgage costs will rise. If bankruptcy judges can rewrite mortgage loans after they are made, it will increase the risk of mortgage lending at the time they are made. Increased risk increases the overall cost of lending, which in turn will require future borrowers to pay higher interest rates and up-front costs, such as higher down payments and points. This is illustrated by a recent example: In 2005, Congress eliminated the power of bankruptcy judges to modify auto loans. A recent staff report by the Federal Reserve Bank of New York estimated a 265 basis-point reduction on average in auto loan terms as a result of the reform.

Allowing mortgage modification in bankruptcy also could unleash a torrent of bankruptcies. To gain a sense of the potential size of the problem, consider that about 800,000 American families filed for bankruptcy in 2007. Rising unemployment and the weakening economy pushed the number near one million in 2008. But by recent count, some five million homeowners are currently delinquent on their mortgages and some 12 million to 15 million homeowners owe more on their mortgages than the home is worth. If even a fraction of those homeowners files for bankruptcy to reduce their interest rates or strip down their principal amounts to the value of their homes, we could see an unprecedented surge in filings, overwhelming the bankruptcy system.

Finally, a bankruptcy proceeding sweeps in all of the filer's other debts, including credit cards, car loans, unpaid medical bills, etc. This means that a surge in new bankruptcy filings, brought about by a judge's power to modify mortgages, could destabilize the market for all other types of consumer credit.

Bankruptcy Abuse

There are other problems. A bankruptcy judge's power to reset interest rates and strip down principal to the value of the property sets up a dynamic that will fail to help many needy homeowners, and also reward bankruptcy abuse.

Consider that the pending legislation requires the judge to set the interest rate at the prime rate plus "a reasonable premium for risk." Question: What is a reasonable risk premium for an already risky subprime borrower who has filed for bankruptcy and is getting the equivalent of a new loan with nothing down?

In a competitive market, such a mortgage would likely fetch a double-digit interest rate—comparable to the rate they already have. Thus, the bankruptcy plan would offer either no relief at all to a subprime borrower, or the bankruptcy judge would set the interest rate at a submarket rate, apparently violating the premise of the statute and piling further harm on the lender.

More worrisome is the opportunity for abuse.

The 2008 Financial Crisis

In financial and economic literature, there are elaborated analyses of the causes of and reasons for the present [2008–2012] global crisis. . . . The critical situation began in the US and was caused when certain homeowners defaulted on the loans extended to them by banks to finance the purchase of their houses. The collateral in the form of mortgages to secure the repayment of these loans appeared to be insufficient. The subsequent loss was not carried by the bank that originally provided the loan, but by other banks and institutions that had 'purchased' the collateralized loans, not in the form of a novation of the contractual relation between the lender and the original bank, but in the form of the purchase of a 'package' of collateralized loans and other financial instruments that through 'securitization' were repackaged in a financial 'product'. The risk profile and other properties of these products were insufficiently clear to the national and international purchasing banks and institutions, which were taken by surprise by the defaults under the original loans causing the products in which they were packaged to lose a substantial part of their value. The national and international trade in these products was extensive enough for these 'bad loans' to result in very serious financial problems for the many banks and institutions that were involved in such trade. These problems then escalated into an economic crisis affecting the global economy.

Bas Steins Bisschop,
"Globalization: Selected Developments in Corporate Law,"
in Globalization and Private Law: The Way Forward.
Eds. Michael Faure and André van der Walt.
Northampton, MA: Edward Elgar Publishing, 2010, pp. 230–231.

Imagine the following situation: A few years ago a borrower took out a $300,000 loan with nothing down to buy a new house. The house rises in value to $400,000, at which time he refinances or takes out a home equity loan to buy a big screen TV and expensive vacations. He still has no equity in the house.

The house subsequently falls in value to $250,000, at which point the borrower files for bankruptcy, the mortgage principal is written down, and the homeowner keeps all the goodies purchased with the home equity loan. Several years from now, however, the house appreciates in value back to $300,000 or more—at which point the homeowner sells the house for a tidy profit.

Nothing in Mr. Conyers' proposed legislation would prevent this scenario from occurring. To modify a mortgage, a borrower would have to enter a Chapter 13 repayment plan for five years. If the homeowner sells his house while he is still in bankruptcy, the mortgage lender can recapture some of any appreciation in its value on a sliding scale—80% the first year, 60% the second, 40% the third, and 20% the fourth. After that, however, any appreciation in the value of the house goes into the debtor's pocket.

This dynamic creates obvious opportunities for borrowers to file for bankruptcy to strip down the value of their property in anticipation of rising real estate markets down the road. At the very least, Congress should extend the time period for allowing lenders to recapture home appreciation beyond five years.

Damage to Credit Markets

Mortgage modifications during bankruptcy will almost certainly increase the losses of mortgage lenders—and this may further freeze credit markets. The reason is that when mortgage-backed securities were created, they provided no allocation of how losses were to be assessed in the event that

Congress would do something inconceivable, such as permitting modification of home mortgages in bankruptcy. According to a Standard & Poor's study, most mortgage-backed securities provide that bankruptcy losses (at least above a certain initial carve out) should be assessed pro rata across all tranches of securities holders. Given the likelihood of an explosion of bankruptcy filings and mortgage losses through bankruptcy, these pro rata sharing provisions likely will be triggered. Thus, the holders of the most senior, lowest-risk tranches would be assessed losses on the same basis as the most junior, riskiest tranches.

The implications of this are obvious and potentially severe: The uncertainty will exacerbate the already existing uncertainty in the financial system, further freezing credit markets.

If Congress wants to deal with the rising number of foreclosures, it should not create a new mess by converting the mortgage crisis into a bankruptcy crisis. Doing so will open the door to a host of unintended consequences that will further freeze credit markets, raise interest rates for new home buyers, and spread the mortgage contagion to other types of consumer credit. Congress needs to reject this plan and look for better solutions.

> *"Having never before dealt with a serious long-term illness, we had no idea how fast those fine-print 'exclusions' could add up."*

The Affordable Care Act Reduces the Threat of Bankruptcy Due to Medical Bills

Matthew Stein

Matthew Stein is an engineer and a building contractor and the author of When Disaster Strikes: A Comprehensive Guide for Emergency Planning and Crisis Survival. *In the following viewpoint, he explains that his finances have been devastated by his wife's cancer diagnosis. Though Stein had health insurance, fine-print exemptions have resulted in huge bills and pushed him to the brink of bankruptcy. He says that the Patient Protection and Affordable Care Act (PPACA), commonly known as the Affordable Care Act (ACA) or Obamacare, is not perfect but that it would save self-employed people from medical bankruptcy.*

As you read, consider the following questions:

1. Why does Stein say he cannot switch health insurance plans?

2. What expenses does the insurance company exclude, according to Stein?

3. How, specifically, will Obamacare help Stein and his wife?

Like millions of others, my wife, Josie, and I are self-employed, middle-class Americans. We are old enough that insurance companies place us in their expensive high-risk categories, but too young to qualify for Medicare.

Not Adequately Covered

Until one of us got really sick, we lived under the illusion that we were adequately covered by our health insurance plan. Two or three months after my wife was diagnosed with cancer, bills from dozens of "excluded" medical expenses started piling up. All those bills had been submitted to our insurance company, and both our medical service providers and ourselves had assumed the insurance company would pay those bills minus the deductibles, and that our in-network and out-of-network caps would apply. Damn those fine-print "exclusions" that I never paid much attention to before!

Unfortunately, by the time we realized how utterly inadequate our health insurance was, we were stuck with it. My wife's cancer is now a serious "preexisting condition," so we don't stand a chance of switching insurance carriers or upgrading our policy, until that day if and when Obamacare [referring to the Patient Protection and Affordable Care Act] becomes a reality. For us, and many thousands of others in similar situations, Obamacare will make the difference between never-ending financial struggles, or having an affordable yet comprehensive health insurance policy along with the prospect for a decent life without fear of bill collectors and bankruptcy.

I am approaching my 57th birthday, and have been exceptionally healthy my entire adult life. Josie turned 63 recently, and up until about one year ago, except for a close call with a deadly toxic mold (*Stachybotrys*) back in 2004, she has also been quite healthy. So much so that I have gone for entire decades without taking as much medication as a single aspirin, and neither of us had previously taken any long-term prescription medications.

As far as our insurance companies were concerned, prior to 2012 we had been the ideal clients—dutifully paying into the system for decades, while almost never drawing funds for claims. Over the past 19 years of self-employment, we have purchased high-deductible "catastrophic coverage" types of health insurance policies to provide medical coverage in case of a serious accident or illness. The unfortunate thing about high-deductible policies like ours is that since you almost never spend enough money on medical expenses to meet the deductible, you have no idea whether or not your insurance coverage is adequate until someone gets seriously sick or severely injured. Once that occurs, you now have a "preexisting" medical condition that makes it nearly impossible to upgrade your health insurance plan, or switch insurance carriers.

Starting in early August of 2012, Josie could feel that something was not right inside her body, so she began an escalating series of medical tests, doctor's visits, and trips to the ER that yielded frustratingly little new information. It was not until shortly after Thanksgiving of 2012 that Josie ended up at the Tahoe Forest Cancer Center where she was properly diagnosed with multiple myeloma—a serious blood-bone cancer that often masquerades with symptoms of various different medical conditions, making it difficult to properly diagnose unless one is a cancer specialist or otherwise intimately familiar with myeloma symptoms. It was not until several months had passed that we started receiving tens of thousands of dollars' worth of medical bills for expenses that our insurance company had refused to pay. Our insurance policy has a $5000 in-network cap and a $10,000 out-of-network cap. In the event of a serious accident or illness, I figured we could handle the $15,000 annual out-of-pocket combined medical expense cap.

Fine-Print Exclusions

Having never before dealt with a serious long-term illness, we had no idea how fast those fine-print "exclusions" could add up. The fine-print exclusions in our medical policy include doctor's visits, prescriptions, and lab work, which, according to my insurance company, also excludes diagnostic tests critical to my wife's medical care, such as monthly tests to track special blood proteins that are myeloma markers, CT scans, X-rays, MRIs, and PET scans. In Josie's case, excluded expenses typically run about $6,000 in a good month, and in bad months those expenses sometimes exceed $12,000! My one-man engineering consulting business generates a decent income, especially when I do not have things like caregiving chores and doctors' visits taking up most of my time, but not the kind of money it takes to cover the extra $100,000+ annually for all those "excluded" medical expenses!

Another option that I have been considering lately is abandoning my consulting business and taking a corporate job in Silicon Valley. Even though I have an impressive resume and an excellent education . . . , at my age (57) it can be quite difficult to secure a good job in the high-tech world, especially once I disclose that my wife is struggling with a life-threatening illness. If successful at securing a suitable corporate position, someone of my caliber will generally be required to put in at least 50 to 60 hours of work each week. This would entail hiring a full-time caregiver for Josie, and vacating our home of 25 years.

The ACA Summarized

In brief, the ACA's [the Affordable Care Act, also known as the Patient Protection and Affordable Care Act or Obamacare] major provisions are as follows (*New York Times* 2010). It is estimated to increase the number of Americans who will have medical care insurance by somewhat over 30 million by 2018, although it will not provide the universal coverage which Canada, for instance, has long provided. Children may no longer be denied insurance coverage on the basis of a preexisting condition, and adults will acquire a similar benefit in 2014. In the interim, the ACA provides a temporary program to help adults with preexisting conditions acquire adequate insurance. The ACA includes a range of other new benefits for Americans who already have insurance, such as allowing their adult children to stay on a family's insurance until age 26 and eliminating lifetime limits on insurance coverage. It creates state-run insurance exchanges to provide affordable group insurance to persons who are self-employed, between jobs or otherwise uninsured. The ACA provides tax benefits to help small businesses buy medical care insurance for their employees. It strengthens Medicare and the insurance coverage it provides in several respects. Other provisions of the ACA are aimed at reducing at least per-unit medical care expenses, although the efficacy of these provisions is hotly contested.

Charles Lockhart,
The Roots of American Exceptionalism:
Institutions, Culture and Policies.
New York: Palgrave MacMillan, 2012.

How many other small business owners across America would face similar gut-wrenching decisions should one of their family members require long-term medical treatment?

Obamacare Is Vital

My wife and I are at that stage in our life when we should be socking away money for our retirement—not worrying about bankruptcy and losing our home. We have paid into the system all our life, but simply because one of us got sick, and we don't happen to have a corporate or government job that provides comprehensive group health insurance coverage, we stand a good chance of losing everything. We live in the richest country in the world, yet millions like ourselves are either uninsured or underinsured, and just one medical catastrophe away from drowning under a mountain of debt. Obamacare is clearly not perfect, but it opens the door for regular folks like us to obtain an affordable comprehensive health insurance plan comparable to those offered to most government and corporate employees, regardless of preexisting conditions or advancing age.

> "The [Patient Protection and] Afford-
> able Care Act will reduce the number
> of uninsured by a little more than half,
> which is a good thing. . . . But it's go-
> ing to increase the problem of underin-
> surance: People who have insurance but
> still can't afford care."

Will Obamacare End Medical Bankruptcies? Probably Not.

Sarah Kliff

Sarah Kliff is a senior editor at Vox and a former reporter at the Washington Post. In the following viewpoint, she argues that the Patient Protection and Affordable Care Act (PPACA), commonly known as the Affordable Care Act (ACA) or Obamacare, will not necessarily end medical bankruptcies. Though the PPACA will insure more people, many of those people may end up underinsured; therefore, that insurance will not pay for all their medical expenses. Kliff points to Massachusetts, which passed a health insurance law similar to the PPACA but did not signifi-cantly cut medical bankruptcies.

As you read, consider the following questions:

1. How many people does Kliff suggest will gain health insurance who did not have it before enactment of the federal health care law?

2. What effect did Stephanie Woolhandler find the Massachusetts health insurance law had on medical bankruptcies?

3. Why might the federal health care law be more effective in reducing bankruptcies than the Massachusetts law, according to Kliff?

There's pretty widespread agreement, on both sides of the aisle, that the health care law will expand insurance coverage. The nonpartisan Congressional Budget Office estimates that 30 million more Americans will have health insurance by the end of a decade. What's become more of a debate though, is how good that health insurance coverage will be. Two new academic studies raise the possibility that many Americans will still face big financial burdens after they gain insurance coverage.

Increased Underinsurance

"The [Patient Protection and] Affordable Care Act will reduce the number of uninsured by a little more than half, which is a good thing," says Stephanie Woolhandler, a professor at the CUNY [City University of New York] School of Public Health. "But it's going to increase the problem of underinsurance: People who have insurance but still can't afford care."

The whole point of buying health insurance coverage is to make care affordable. Millions of Americans pay monthly premiums with the expectation that, should a horrible illness or accident occur, the insurance company will cover the majority of some pretty expensive hospital bills.

Some experts and health advocates have begun to question whether the health care law can deliver on that promise. Woolhandler wrote an editorial earlier this week [in April 2013], in the *Journal of General Internal Medicine*, contending that "the new private coverage offered to the near-poor and middle income individuals through insurance exchanges will also leave many underinsured."

Much of this has to do with the type of plans that insurers will sell on the health insurance exchange. Health insurers will offer consumers a "bronze" plan that will, on average, cover 60 percent of an enrollee's costs. This, in health insurance–speak, is known as "actuarial value." Using actuarial values can make it easier to compare plans and understand what part of the bill the insurer will likely cover—and how much the enrollee can expect to be on the hook to pay.

The exchange will also have other plans with different actuarial values: Silver plans will cover 70 percent of an average enrollee's costs, and gold plans would be expected to foot 80 percent of the bill. The bronze plans are expected to attract a high number of enrollees, since they will likely have smaller premiums—because consumers are buying less robust financial coverage.

Woolhandler, who is the cofounder of Physicians for a National Health Program, has previously conducted research on rates of medical bankruptcy in Massachusetts, before and after the state expanded health insurance access. She found that in 2009, two years after the insurance expansion took effect, just about half the debtors (52 percent) attributed their bankruptcy at least in part to medical bills. In 2007, before the expansion, the number stood at 59 percent.

Alison Galbraith, an assistant professor at Harvard Medical School, has also looked at Massachusetts's insurance expansion to better understand how access to health insurance affects the financial burden of medical costs.

She published a paper this month in the journal *Health Affairs*, which looked at which costs were faced by families who had gained insurance through the [Health] Connector,

Massachusetts's version of a health care exchange. She found that 38 percent reported a financial burden (defined as having difficulty paying medical bills) and 45 percent said costs were higher than they had expected.

Numbers were slightly higher for those earning less than 400 percent of the poverty line and for those with children.

Better than Massachusetts?

It's worth noting that the Massachusetts bronze plans had a lower actuarial value than those that will be sold on the exchanges. They covered, on average, 40 to 50 percent of enrollees' costs. That means, to Galbraith, that underinsurance is still a concern in the federal exchanges—but perhaps not as much as it has been in the Massachusetts experience.

"The exchanges will provide coverage and that will help the uninsured but there's still an underinsured problem," Galbraith says. "People will have plans, but they will still have cost issues involved."

Galbraith contends that this creates an impetus for better consumer education—that there's space for better education about how much health insurance will cover, and what consumers might be expected to pay. Some employers, for example, will provide cost calculators where enrollees can input some data on what type of health care spending they expect and get a sense of which plan might provide the best deal.

That can move consumers away from just comparing premiums, and toward thinking about all the *other* costs they could incur from various co-payments and cost-sharing. That could lead consumers to pick different plans, which might come with higher premiums—but also lower cost-sharing down the line.

Periodical and Internet Sources Bibliography

The following articles have been selected to supplement the diverse views presented in this chapter.

Paul Abrams	"Affordable Care Act Insures Against Illness AND Bankruptcy," *Daily Kos*, November 6, 2013.
Patrick Clark	"You Can Get Student Loans Forgiven in Bankruptcy, but It's Far from Easy," *Bloomberg Businessweek*, May 6, 2014.
Amilda Dymi	"Foreclosure 70% Less Likely for Homeowners Filing Bankruptcy: Study," *American Banker*, May 23, 2014.
Tyler Kingkade	"Bankruptcy Should Be an Option for Some Student Loans: Report," *Huffington Post*, August 20, 2013.
Dan Mangan	"Medication Costs Fuel Painful Medical Debt, Bankruptcies," CNBC, May 28, 2014.
Josh Mitchell	"Harkin Opens Door to Bankruptcy Option for Student Loans," *Wall Street Journal*, June 25, 2014.
Kerri Anne Renzulli	"What Congress Should Do to Give Student Loan Borrowers Hope for Relief," *Time*, October 15, 2014.
Steve Rhode	"4 Out of 10 Actually Were Able to Discharge Student Loans in Bankruptcy—But Most Never Try," *Huffington Post*, January 7, 2013.
Katy Stech	"5 Things Student Loan Lawyers Ask Borrowers Who File for Bankruptcy," *Wall Street Journal*, January 6, 2014.
Today	"Biggest Cause of Personal Bankruptcy: Medical Bills," June 25, 2013.

CHAPTER 3

What Are Issues Facing Cities That Declare Bankruptcy?

Chapter Preface

When Detroit filed for bankruptcy in 2013, it was the biggest municipality ever to seek bankruptcy protection. Until then, that dubious honor had belonged to Jefferson County, Alabama, which contains the city of Birmingham. Following the financial crisis in 2008, Jefferson County found itself unable to pay its creditors and sought bankruptcy protection in 2011. It exited bankruptcy in 2013. While creditors forgave $1.4 billion in debt, the city still owes $1.8 billion, which it hopes to pay back in a forty-year plan.

So now that it is no longer bankrupt, is Jefferson County healthy and solvent again? Commenters disagree on the subject. Martin Z. Braun in a November 23, 2013, article for Bloomberg quotes Matt Fabian of Municipal Market Advisors who explains that "there's a lot of pain going around—bondholders are taking large losses, but ratepayers are as well." In particular, Braun says, the county's already high sewer rates are to rise 7.9 percent for four years and another 3.5 percent every year through 2053. This is on top of a more than 325 percent rate increase in the years before the bankruptcy. Overall, in principal and interest, residents and businesses will end up paying back more to creditors than what they owed before the bankruptcy. Nor is the county out of trouble; future forecasts show "a projected $1.2 billion gap in money available to maintain the sewer system," according to Braun.

In a December 5, 2013, article in *Forbes*, Dan Alexander points out that, despite ongoing troubles, there are some promising signs in Jefferson County as well. Birmingham's economy is undergoing a strong recovery, fueled by hiring in automobile manufacturing and a new American Cast Iron Pipe Company facility. The University of Birmingham at Alabama (UAB) received $172 million in research funding from the National Institutes of Health, and its research contracts and expansion have helped boost the city as a whole. For example, UAB and the city and county worked together to create a "business incubator"; according to Alexander, "The Innovation Depot now houses roughly 500 employees working for 95 different companies."

The authors of the viewpoints in the following chapter examine other important municipal bankruptcies, including the bankruptcy of a number of cities in California, to determine issues that financially stress cities.

| "We got reform. We just got it a different way than everybody wanted."

RPT-Stockton Sales Tax Plan Set to End Bankruptcy, Pensions Spared

Jim Christie

Jim Christie is a journalist at Reuters. In the following viewpoint, he reports that Stockton, California, was forced into bankruptcy. Creditors wanted to rework and decrease the city's pension obligations and initially refused to negotiate without changes to pensions. However, a bankruptcy judge declared that the refusal to negotiate was in bad faith. Eventually, Christie explains, Stockton renegotiated with its creditors, retained its pension benefits, and reduced its liabilities in part by reworking health care benefits.

As you read, consider the following questions:

1. What tax changes does Christie say Stockton undertook to get out of bankruptcy?

2. What does the California Constitution say about pensions and bankruptcy?

3. What does Christie say Stockton will have to do if voters reject the bankruptcy plan?

When Stockton, California, filed for bankruptcy last year [2012], the stage was set for a precedent-setting battle with Wall Street over whether bondholders or retired public employees should pay the price when a local government goes broke.

A Speedy Conclusion

But under the terms of recent settlements, bond insurers who are backing about $240 million in city debt will accept a "haircut" of as much as 50 percent on some bonds. Retirees will keep their full pensions, though 1,100 of them will lose their retiree health insurance.

On Tuesday [November 5, 2013], Stockton voters are likely to approve a sales tax increase that could all but seal a surprisingly speedy end to the city's bankruptcy case. With that, the much-anticipated showdown over pensions will move to Detroit or another city seeking court protection from creditors.

Massive cuts to Stockton's budget will remain. The sales tax increase will raise about $300 million over 10 years and likely enable the city to emerge from bankruptcy early next year.

"We got reform. We just got it a different way than everybody wanted," said City Manager Bob Deis, who recently retired and is credited with driving a tough but well-organized bankruptcy process.

He said polls showed 60 percent of voters supported the tax hike, which would raise Stockton's sales tax to 9 percent from 8.25 percent, which includes the state sales tax of 7.5 percent.

For troubled municipalities and their lenders, the lessons from Stockton are mixed.

From one perspective, the case suggests trying to force a showdown on pensions may not be a good strategy for Wall Street. Legal experts say Stockton's biggest bond insurers, Assured Guaranty and National Public Finance Guarantee, overplayed their hand by demanding that pensions be on the table before they would even negotiate.

Further, Stockton was reluctant to test a provision of the state constitution that its pension fund, the California Public Employees' Retirement System (CalPERS), argues protects pension payments even in the event of a bankruptcy. Instead, retirees were asked to share the pain by losing their health insurance, a step the city could take without a protracted legal battle and one that slashed its long-term liabilities by $500 million.

"When you're in the middle of a restructuring, you tend to move to things that have clarity," said Karol Denniston, a San Francisco lawyer who helped write the California law guiding municipal bankruptcies.

Yet the question of whether pensions can be cut in the face of a municipal fiscal crisis is not likely to go away.

In Detroit's bankruptcy case, a similar battle is brewing over whether state law protecting pensions can be trumped in federal bankruptcy court. Given that city's massive pension liabilities, it is not clear that a Stockton-style solution would be possible.

In San Bernardino, California's bankruptcy, the city stopped making its bimonthly payments to CalPERS for a full year and is now $17 million behind on its current obligations. CalPERS is fighting the city's bankruptcy tactics on every legal front.

In the meantime, the city of San Jose, California, is fighting a lawsuit over its move to alter how current employees earn pension benefits. San Jose mayor Chuck Reed is spearheading a state-wide ballot initiative to clear any legal roadblocks to such efforts.

Cuts, Then Bankruptcy

Stockton filed its petition for bankruptcy protection last year after drastic cutbacks—including furloughs, pay cuts and a 40 percent reduction in its payroll—failed to keep its budget in balance. The city was reeling from a plunge in tax revenues caused by the recession and the implosion of a once-hot housing market, on top of ill-conceived spending on projects such as a downtown sports arena.

Deis, who arrived in 2010 after working as the administrator of Sonoma County, California, led the restructuring effort. Even after all the belt-tightening, Deis in early 2012 took more drastic actions, including defaulting on some debt and launching talks with creditors in hopes of staving off bankruptcy.

Negotiations failed, and on June 28, 2012, Stockton filed for bankruptcy—the biggest U.S. city to do so until Detroit took away that dubious crown earlier this year.

Reflecting the concern that Stockton could set a precedent with broad implications for the municipal debt market, Stockton's bond insurers, Assured Guaranty and National Public Finance Guarantee, aggressively challenged the city's eligibility for bankruptcy. They insisted the city could simply cut services further—a position that led Deis to accuse them of advocating "anarchy in the streets," since police are the main cost in the crime-plagued city.

The attack on Stockton's eligibility backfired.

U.S. bankruptcy judge Christopher Klein had at one point suggested that it would be hard to resolve the case without pensions being part of the discussion. In his ruling in June affirming Stockton's eligibility, however, he hammered Assured and National on several fronts.

Klein said the bond insurers had not bargained in good faith by assuming a "we-have-nothing-to-talk-about position" when the city indicated it would not go after pension payments.

He also detailed Stockton's successful talks with other creditors and the painful measures, including dumping retiree health insurance, that it had agreed to take. He also noted that the city's deals with employees would indirectly reduce its pension obligations over the long run.

Any complaints about pensions would need to be raised later, in proceedings over the confirmation of the final plan to exit bankruptcy, Klein added.

The stinging loss gave the creditors an incentive to negotiate with Stockton, said David Mastagni, a Sacramento lawyer for Stockton's police officers who over the past year has struck deals with the city on officers' pay and pensions.

The creditors relied on "political theater," Mastagni said. "That's why the decision was so harsh."

Klein's decision marked an important lesson about Chapter 9 proceedings, said municipal bankruptcy expert Denniston: "The eligibility process is meant just for eligibility, not setting the table for other issues."

Heading for the Exit

Tuesday's vote is the last key piece of Deis' plan for exiting bankruptcy. If voters balk, Stockton will have to close libraries, recreation centers and firehouses—and reopen talks with its creditors.

Even with new revenue, the city will need to keep a lid on most spending, though the measure specifically includes funding to hire more than 100 additional police officers.

A formal exit from bankruptcy does not mean the city's fiscal troubles are over. In Vallejo, a San Francisco Bay Area city that filed for bankruptcy in 2008 and pursued a restructuring similar to Stockton's, the budget is again out of balance just two years after the city emerged from Chapter 9.

Stockton is counting on a housing recovery and continued improvement in the economy to make it all work.

"Until we do get a full recovery, a lot of cities are going to be grasping at straws and gasping," said Steven Frates, research director at Pepperdine University's School of Public Policy.

For Stockton's residents, glimmers of hope are mixed with weary resignation.

Jodi Anderson, a 47-year-old retired police dispatcher, said she would vote for Stockton's tax hike, even though she has already involuntarily helped the city's restructuring.

"The city won't get out of bankruptcy without it. . . . I don't want to start from scratch again," she said. Anderson has gone without health insurance for more than a year, along with her husband Mark, a 54-year-old retired police officer.

Both believed their medical coverage would be rock-solid despite the city's weakening finances.

"We knew there were drastic things on the horizon but we didn't envision bankruptcy," Anderson said.

> *"For anyone who cares about govern-
> ment and wants government to suc-
> ceed, the pension problem must be ad-
> dressed, for it threatens not only
> economic disaster, but political cyni-
> cism beyond even today's wildest
> dreams."*

Cities Must Confront Public Pensions to Solve Fiscal Problems

Roger Berkowitz

*Roger Berkowitz is the academic director of the Hannah Arendt
Center for Politics and Humanities at Bard College. In the following viewpoint, he argues that cities are unable to fund their
pension obligations. He says that this is a serious problem because it forces cities into bankruptcy and that in turn requires
intervention by state or federal governments, reducing local au-
tonomy. He also says pensions will inevitably need to be ad-
justed; therefore, it is vital that cities stop misleading pension re-
cipients about their eventual benefits. He concludes that pensions
must be reorganized as soon as possible.*

Roger Berkowitz, "The Pension Crisis in Cities," Hannah Arendt Center, January 17,
2013. © 2013 Hannah Arendt Center. All rights reserved. Reproduced by permission.

As you read, consider the following questions:

1. According to Berkowitz, how did pension funding fall between 2007 and 2009?

2. Why does Berkowitz say it is important to pay attention to problems in cities in particular as opposed to states?

3. What does Berkowitz say will happen as government services are hollowed out in response to the pension crisis?

The Pew Center on the States issued a study this week [in January 2013] that sheds further light on our municipal pension problems, a political crisis with strong Arendtian [referring to philosopher Hannah Arendt] overtones. Where most studies have focused on the enormous problems faced by states, this one focuses on cities:

> Cities employing nearly half of U.S. municipal workers saw their pension and retiree health-care funding levels fall from 79% in fiscal year 2007 to 74% in fiscal year 2009, using the latest available data, according to the Pew Center on the States. Pension systems are considered healthy if they are 80% funded.
>
> The growing funding gulf, which the study estimated at more than $217 billion for the 61 cities in the study, raises worries about local finances at a time when states are also struggling to recover from the recession. Property-tax revenue dipped during the housing crisis, straining city finances amid a weak national economy.

Cities and Pensions

The reason to pay attention to the problems in cities is that cities have even less ability to solve their pension shortfalls than states. The smaller the population, the more a city would have to tax each citizen in order to help pay for the pensions of its retired public workers. The result is that either cities get bailed out by states and lose their independence (as is happening in Michigan) or the cities file for bankruptcy (as is happening in California).

Also this week the *New York Times* ran a story about San Bernardino, one of three California cities to file for bankruptcy as a result of their pension obligations. It is a stark reminder of why we should care about public pensions:

> Five months after San Bernardino filed for bankruptcy—the third California city to seek Chapter 9 protections in 2012— residents here are confronting a transformed and more perilous city. After violent crime had dropped steadily for years, the homicide rate shot up more than 50 percent in 2012 as a shrinking police force struggled to keep order in a city long troubled by street gangs that have migrated from Los Angeles, 60 miles to the west.... "The parks department is shredded, the libraries similarly," [the mayor] said. "My office is down to nobody. I've got literally no one left."

A similar fate is befalling other California cities that are in bankruptcy:

> Stockton, Calif., which filed for bankruptcy in June [2013], has followed a similarly grim path into insolvency, logging more homicides last year than ever before. In Vallejo, Calif., which filed for bankruptcy in 2008, cuts left the police force a third smaller, and the city became a hub for prostitution.

As I have argued, the pension crisis is not arcane policy or economics. It is a crisis of politics and government. It came about because municipal and state governments offered irresponsible contracts to public employees. There is no way these contractually guaranteed pensions can be paid. By refusing to face up to this fact now, we are making the problem worse. The result will be the hollowing out of local government services across the country. Police forces will be decimated. Public libraries and fire stations will close. Parks will fall into dis-

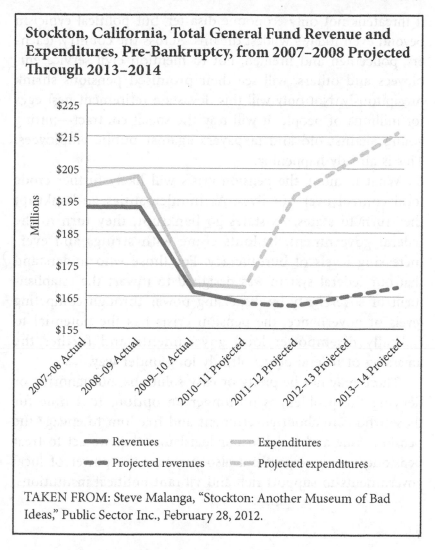

Stockton, California, Total General Fund Revenue and Expenditures, Pre-Bankruptcy, from 2007–2008 Projected Through 2013–2014

TAKEN FROM: Steve Malanga, "Stockton: Another Museum of Bad Ideas," Public Sector Inc., February 28, 2012.

repair. All in order to pay full pensions to retirees. This of course won't happen. Cities will refuse to do it, as they have in California and elsewhere. The result will then be bankruptcy, which comes with its own tragedies.

Pensions Must Be Addressed

For anyone who cares about government and wants government to succeed, the pension problem must be addressed, for it threatens not only economic disaster, but political cynicism beyond even today's wildest dreams. Across the country, teachers, policemen and firemen, not to mention civil service employees and others, will see their promised pensions shrink precipitously. Not only will this devastate retirement nest eggs for millions of people, it will fray the social contract—pitting young against old and taxpayers against public employees. This is already happening.

What is more, the pension crisis will likely further erode local control over our lives. As municipalities go bankrupt they turn to states. As states go bankrupt, they turn to the federal government. Bailouts come with strings and ever-increasing levels of bureaucracy. For those who understand that our federal system was designed to thwart the establishment of sovereignty by dispersing power through competing levels of governance, the pension crisis has the potential to radically disempower local governments and further the amassing of federal power already long under way.

There may not be pretty or easy solutions, but ignoring or denying the problem is no longer an option. It is time for those who care about government and freedom to engage the pension issue and insist to our legislators that we act to treat pensioners with respect but also preserve the power of local governments to support rich and vibrant political institutions.

> "Assistant City Manager Craig Whittom, who has worked in Vallejo since 2003, said the bankruptcy may have been the best thing to happen."

Vallejo, Calif., Once Bankrupt, Is Now a Model for Cities in an Age of Austerity

Ariana Eunjung Cha

Ariana Eunjung Cha is a staff writer at the Washington Post. *In the following viewpoint, she reports on Vallejo, California, which declared bankruptcy in 2008. While the initial effects of the bankruptcy were detrimental, as crime surged, in the long term the bankruptcy has been good for the city. Released from its debts, Vallejo was able to reorganize, investing in high-tech equipment to improve policing and to keep costs down over the long term, as well as partnering with citizens in innovative ways. Cha says that city officials see the bankruptcy as a positive experience and are pleased that Vallejo is on much firmer financial footing than many other California cities.*

As you read, consider the following questions:

1. What made the first couple of years after bankruptcy ugly in Vallejo, according to Cha?

2. How does Cha say Vallejo addressed policing following the bankruptcy?

3. What experiment in participatory budgeting did Vallejo try, according to Cha?

The first couple of years were ugly. After this working-class port city became the largest in America to declare bankruptcy in 2008, crime and prostitution surged as the police force was thinned by 40 percent. Firehouses were shuttered, and funding for libraries and senior centers was slashed. Foreclosures multiplied and home prices plummeted.

Reinvention

But then this city of 116,000 began to reinvent itself. It started using technology to fill personnel gaps, rallying residents to volunteer to provide public services and offering local voters the chance to decide how money would be spent—in return for an increase in the sales tax. For the first time in five years, the city expects to have enough money to do such things as fill potholes, clear weeds, trim trees and repair tennis courts. The nation's cities are weak links in the U.S. economy and, if they collapse in large numbers, it could knock the country's recovery off course. Cuts at the federal level are being pushed down to the states, which in turn are passing the problems to their cities. The strains are especially great in California, which was at the epicenter of the housing market meltdown and the deep recession that followed. Even before revenue slowed, the state was facing unique constraints on public finances because its laws make it difficult to raise taxes.

The dire conditions, however, have made California a laboratory for how to run cities in an age of austerity.

Declaring bankruptcy used to be a last resort for cities, not only because it would cripple their ability to borrow for years to come but because of the blow to their reputation. But that attitude has started to change as more cities have found themselves facing fiscal catastrophe; bankruptcy offers an opportunity to start over with a clean slate.

At least three California cities—Stockton, Mammoth Lakes and Montebello—have declared that they are exploring the option. And at least 100 of the state's 482 cities are on track to face a similar predicament by the end of the year, according to Barbara O'Connor, a professor at California State University at Sacramento.

Chris McKenzie, executive director of the League of California Cities, said that "no one expected the downturn to last this long," adding: "After years of struggling to keep things together as best they could, cities are getting closer and closer to the edge."

Economists warn that a number of large bankruptcies of cities, concentrated over a short period of time, could have a devastating effect on the national economy. Banking analyst Meredith Whitney in 2010 ominously predicted hundreds of billions of dollars in municipal bond defaults. While defaults on that scale haven't happened—and Whitney's critics came out in droves to attest to the health of the municipal bond market—the specter of such a crisis hasn't disappeared.

City's Cash Runs Out

Vallejo, about 35 miles northeast of San Francisco, became the poster child for the failures of municipal budgeting in 2008 when its cash reserves dwindled to zero and it was unable to pay its bills amid falling property tax revenue and the soaring cost of employee compensation and pensions.

During happier times, Vallejo's salaries for city employees had ballooned, with a number of top officials making $200,000 or $300,000. More than 80 percent of the municipal budget went toward compensation.

The city's credit rating dropped to junk status, and as part of its bankruptcy settlement, Vallejo paid only five cents for every dollar it owed to bondholders. On the labor side, officials cut workers' pay, health care and other benefits but left pensions intact.

For Vallejo to survive, two city council members—Marti Brown, 46, a redevelopment worker for the state, and Stephanie Gomes, 45, a legislative specialist for the U.S. Forest Service—decided that the city needed to study best practices from around the world and bring some of them to California.

"We're trying to be more innovative and risk-taking," Brown said. "It's something we've been forced to do, but it's turning out to be a really positive experience for the city." The police went high-tech, investing $500,000 in cameras across the city that allow officers to monitor a larger area than they could before. The department deputized citizens to participate in law enforcement by sharing tips on Facebook and Twitter. Gomes, whose husband is a retired police officer, focused on public safety. The couple went neighborhood to neighborhood setting up e-mail groups and social media accounts so people can, for instance, share pictures of suspicious vehicles and other information. "There have been countless cases where ordinary people have stopped crimes this way," Gomes said.

The number of neighborhood watch groups jumped from 15 to 350. Citizen volunteers came together monthly to paint over graffiti and do other cleanup work.

And the city council struck an unusual deal with residents—if they agreed to a one-penny sales tax increase, projected to generate an additional $9.5 million in revenue, they could vote on how the money would be used. The experiment in participatory budgeting, which began in April [2012], is the first in a North American city.

The approach was pioneered in Porto Alegre, Brazil, as a way to get citizens involved in bridging the large gap between the city's middle-class residents and those living in slums on the outskirts. Individual districts in New York and Chicago are also experimenting with the process, and residents there have expressed interest in spending money on things such as more security cameras and lighting, public murals, and Meals on Wheels for seniors.

A Statewide Shortfall

As the 2012–13 budget season kicks off in California, Vallejo's neighbors are looking at severe cuts, in part because of reduced support from the state. Gov. Jerry Brown (D) this month revealed that California is facing a crushing $16 billion deficit because of a shortfall in tax revenue. As a result, the state is diverting billions that had been earmarked for redevelopment or housing assistance away from cities that were already under fiscal stress.

Stockton is in eleventh-hour negotiations with creditors to try to avoid bankruptcy. The city of Hercules defaulted on a $2.4 million bond interest payment in February. Vacaville is considering closing City Hall every Friday and forcing employees to take unpaid leave or vacation time.

The state capital, Sacramento, which is expecting an $18 million deficit for fiscal 2012–13, has proposed cutting 286 full-time jobs, including police and firefighters, a move that would probably leave the city unable to respond to home burglaries and car accidents and lengthen the response time for 911 calls in all but the most dire cases.

Vallejo is in a markedly different situation. While it still faces some serious challenges—crime continues to be a problem, and the housing market remains depressed—the city's finances are doing so well that a federal judge released it from bankruptcy in November. "We're seeing a lot of cities around us that are where we were five years ago," Gomes said. "Some of those cities were laughing at us back then. It's nice to be on the other side of it."

While its general-fund budget of $69 million for 2012–13 is a far cry from the $85 million at its peak in the 1980s, Vallejo is in much better financial shape than many other cities around the country.

Assistant City Manager Craig Whittom, who has worked in Vallejo since 2003, said the bankruptcy may have been the best thing to happen: "It was effective at helping us recreate ourselves and change the culture so that we could restart from a stronger financial footing."

> *"The main culprit: Ballooning pension costs, which will hit more than $14 million this year, a nearly 40% increase from two years ago."*

Once Bankrupt, Vallejo Still Can't Afford Its Pricey Pensions

Melanie Hicken

Melanie Hicken is a personal finance reporter at CNN Money. In the following viewpoint, she reports that Vallejo, California, continues to struggle financially after its bankruptcy. She says that while tax hikes and reduced services have helped with budget shortfalls, the main problem remains pensions. Vallejo did not reduce pension benefits during bankruptcy, and it still has serious problems making payments. Hicken concludes that addressing pension payments is necessary if the city is to deal with its long-term financial problems and not enter bankruptcy again.

As you read, consider the following questions:

1. According to Hicken, what are the retirement benefits for Vallejo police and firefighters?

2. How does Hicken say Vallejo reacted to the housing boom?

3. What is CalPERS's position on pensions and bankruptcy?

The California city of Vallejo emerged from bankruptcy just over two years ago, but it is still struggling to pay its bills.

Pension Problems

The main culprit: Ballooning pension costs, which will hit more than $14 million this year, a nearly 40% increase from two years ago.

Amid threats of legal action from the state's pension giant, CalPERS [California Public Employees' Retirement System], Vallejo did little during its nearly three-year stint in bankruptcy to stem the growth in its pension bills.

As a result, Vallejo continues to dole out large sums of money for retirees. Except for new hires, Vallejo's police and firefighters can retire at age 50 with as much as 90% of their salary—for life. Public safety workers who retired in the last five years have average annual pensions of more than $101,000.

And the pension costs are expected to continue to rise, with a projected increase of up to 42% over the next five years.

Moody's recently warned that Vallejo's pension obligations could force it to file for bankruptcy protection a second time. The credit rating agency said the city offers a cautionary tale for two other California cities teetering on the brink: San Bernardino and Stockton.

Vallejo City Manager Dan Keen counters that the city's financial position isn't as bleak as Moody's says. He said the city is in a much "better place" than when it filed for bank-

The Stigma of Municipal Bankruptcy

Dan Keen knew what he was getting into when he took the post of city manager of Vallejo, Calif., more than a year ago. Keen understood that Vallejo, a city of more than 100,000 people about 30 miles north of San Francisco, had just emerged from a grueling three-year bankruptcy case. The working-class port town had become the largest municipality to file for bankruptcy after it ran out of money in May 2008. Unable to pay its bills, Vallejo faced a $16 million deficit amid falling property tax revenue and soaring costs in employee compensation and pensions.

So when Keen arrived in Vallejo, he fully expected plenty of headaches. But it was the little things that got him.

"When I came here, the copy machine was on the fritz," Keen says. "As opposed to leasing a new copy machine, which you would do in other cities, that's not an option in Vallejo because they're not going to lease to you. You're a bankrupt city."

Liz Farmer, "The 'B' Word:
Is Municipal Bankruptcy's Stigma Fading?," in
State and Local Government: 2013–2014 Edition.
Eds. Kevin B. Smith and Jayme Neiman.
Thousand Oaks, CA: SAGE, 2014, p.165.

ruptcy, in part due to a 1% sales tax hike that is funding new city services, like the installation of new surveillance cameras aimed at improving public safety.

In addition, employee concessions, such as a 5% pay cut for police, will allow the city to fill this year's projected $5.2 million budget shortfall, he said.

Still, Keen said pension costs are a major concern.

"If we don't resolve those costs, then we're going to see services continue to suffer," said Keen, who has led the city since 2012. "We're going to have to cut somewhere."

A lot of cuts have already been made.

Vallejo's roads are littered with potholes. Three of its nine fire stations remain closed. And its police force is down by almost 40%—though Keen says there are plans to hire more officers this year.

Crime

Crime has surged, with more than two dozen homicides last year, compared to only seven in 2006. Burglaries are also on the rise. Residents maintain neighborhood watch groups, but the crime is taking a toll.

"Some people in my neighborhood are voting with their feet and leaving Vallejo," resident Russell Zellers wrote in a 2013 letter to City Hall. "If things continue along the present course, I may not be far behind them."

In the fatter years, Vallejo enjoyed a housing boom like many California cities. Flush with property tax revenues, city leaders approved increases in salaries and benefits for city workers. Police officers and firefighters were earning six-figure salaries, even before overtime.

As costs grew, city officials began dipping into the city's cash reserves to pay the bills. Then, in May 2008, after a wave of foreclosures caused property tax revenue to plummet, the city could no longer afford the generous salaries and other benefits it was paying and was forced to file for bankruptcy.

To help cut its debt, the city slashed retiree health benefits and the interest payments it paid to banks. It also cut pension benefits for new hires and raised the amount current workers must contribute to their pensions. But it did not attempt to cut pension benefits for current workers and retirees, a move that can only be attempted during bankruptcy.

In its report, Moody's blamed the state's pension giant CalPERS for Vallejo's lack of action.

CalPERS, which manages $277 billion in retirement assets for more than 1.6 million workers and retirees, has repeatedly argued that pension benefits are protected by California law. It says it is an "arm of the state" and should therefore be exempt from bankruptcy proceedings—meaning it should get paid in full while other creditors could get pennies on the dollar.

Workers and retirees say their pensions were promised through employment contracts and they shouldn't be penalized for the city's bad planning.

So far, no bankrupt California city has ever challenged CalPERS over pension cuts. CalPERS did not respond to a request for comment.

Vallejo's bankruptcy was likely only a short-term fix to its financial problems, said Michael Sweet, a California-based bankruptcy attorney at Fox Rothschild LLP.

"The problem will continue to fester until people face up to the fact that the money available is less than promises made," he said.

Periodical and Internet Sources Bibliography

The following articles have been selected to supplement the diverse views presented in this chapter.

Bob Adelmann	"Vallejo, California, Likely Headed for Second Bankruptcy," *New American*, March 17, 2014.
Michael A. Fletcher	"In San Jose, Generous Pensions for City Workers Come at Expense of Nearly All Else," *Washington Post*, February 25, 2014.
John Gallagher	"Public Pension Reform in Detroit: Many Options—and All of Them Painful," *Detroit Free Press*, March 2, 2014.
Jennifer G. Hickey	"Coming Pension Meltdown: The 10 Most Troubled City Systems," Newsmax, November 11, 2013.
Rick Lyman and Mary Williams Walsh	"Police Salaries and Pensions Push California City to Brink," *New York Times*, December 28, 2013.
Alicia H. Munnell, Jean-Pierre Aubry, Josh Hurwitz, and Mark Cafarelli	"Gauging the Burden of Public Pensions on Cities," Center for Retirement Research, November 2013.
James Nash	"Desert Hot Springs Debates Police Versus Bankruptcy Path," Bloomberg, June 18, 2014.
PBS Newshour	"Cities in Financial Straits Weigh Bankruptcy," February 8, 2014.
Brad Plumer	"Detroit Isn't Alone. The U.S. Cities That Have Gone Bankrupt, in One Map," *Washington Post*, July 18, 2013.
Mary Williams Walsh	"Detroit Rolls Out New Model: A Hybrid Pension Plan," *New York Times*, June 18, 2014.

When Are Government Bailouts Preferable to Bankruptcy?

Chapter Preface

Following the financial crisis of 2008, the federal government provided controversial bailout packages to a number of financial institutions, totaling billions of dollars. This was far from the first time that the government had bailed out failed banks, however. Just twenty years before, in the early 1990s, the United States paid out even more money to prop up the failing savings and loan (S&L) industry.

In a September 25, 2008, article at *Mother Jones*, James Ridgeway argues that the savings and loan crisis was very similar to the mortgage crisis of 2008. According to Ridgeway,

> A flurry of deregulation gave S&Ls the capabilities of major commercial banks without the corresponding oversight and regulation. S&Ls proceeded to make high-risk investments, including thousands of unsound mortgages during a housing boom. The government looked away—until the bottom fell out and the S&Ls started to fall like dominoes. Then it stepped in with a bailout of then-unprecedented levels, which added to ballooning deficits and ushered in years of recession.

There were differences between the two rounds of bailouts as well, however. First, the savings and loan bailout cost considerably more. The 2008 bailout is estimated to end up costing around $65 billion, according to Mark Gongloff in a January 1, 2013, article in the *Huffington Post*. The savings and loan bailout, on the other hand, cost about $220 billion, according to Peter Cohan in a July 3, 2010, article on the DailyFinance website. Both crises touched off serious recessions. However, the 2008 recession was much worse; it did much more damage in terms of lost jobs and lost productivity. While the government paid less in bailout money in 2008 than it had in the early 1990s, the 2008 financial crisis was ultimately more damaging and more costly.

Has America learned how to avoid these kinds of disastrous financial meltdowns in the future? Cohan is skeptical. He argues that the government still has not put limits on Wall Street borrowing and that financial institutions still have incentives to engage in risky behavior for large returns. "Until our laws reflect those lessons," Cohan says, "we are doomed to repeat the mistakes of economic history."

The authors in the following chapter discuss controversies surrounding bailouts of the automobile industry and financial institutions such as AIG and ponder whether it was wise for the government to bail out these institutions rather than let them go bankrupt.

"Keeping the government's tentacles around a large firm in an important industry will keep the door open wider to industrial policy and will deter market-driven decision making throughout the industry, possibly keeping the brakes on the recovery."

Bankruptcy, Not Government Bailouts, Would Have Been Best for the Auto Industry

Daniel J. Ikenson

Daniel J. Ikenson is director of the Herbert A. Stiefel Center for Trade Policy Studies at the Cato Institute. In the following viewpoint, he argues that the bailout of the automobile industry following the 2008 financial collapse was a failure. He says that the claim that the auto industry would collapse was overblown. He adds that government intervention cost taxpayers billions and led to distortions in the market. In particular, he says, the auto industry has too much capacity, and the bailout prevented a reorganization, bilking stockholders, creditors, and competitors

Daniel J. Ikenson, "Lasting Implications of the General Motors Bailout," Cato Institute, June 22, 2011. © 2011 The Cato Institute. All rights reserved. Reproduced by permission.

who had run their businesses better than the automakers who were bailed out. He also says that the bailout undermined the rule of law and faith in the market.

As you read, consider the following questions:

1. According to Ikenson, how did the chairmen of the automakers lay waste to months of public relations planning?

2. Why does Ikenson say he views the fate of General Motors (GM) as a matter of national indifference?

3. What does Ikenson say is the most significant factor suppressing the stock value of GM?

On November 5, 2008, the Center for Automotive Research [CAR], a Detroit-based consulting firm, released the results of a study warning that as many as three million jobs were at stake in the automotive sector unless the U.S. government acted with dispatch to ensure the continued operation of all of the Big Three automakers [General Motors Company (GM), Ford Motor Company, and Chrysler Group]. Detroit's media blitz was under way. It was timed to remind then president-elect [Barack] Obama, as he contemplated his victory the morning after, of the contribution to his success by certain constituencies now seeking assistance themselves. The CAR report's projection of three million lost jobs was predicated on the fantastical worst-case scenario that if one of the Big Three were to go out of business and liquidate, numerous firms in the auto supply chain would go under as well, bringing down the remaining two Detroit auto producers, then the foreign nameplate U.S. producers and the rest of the parts supply chain. The job loss projections animating the national discussion were based on an assumption of a total loss of all automobile and auto parts production and sales jobs nationwide. Importantly, the report gave no consideration to the more realistic scenario that one or two of the Detroit automakers might seek Chapter 11 protection to reorganize.

Crisis-Mongering

The subsequent public relations effort to make the case for federal assistance was pitched in a crisis atmosphere with an air of certainty that the only real alternative to massive federal assistance was liquidation and contagion. The crisis-mongering was reminiscent of former treasury secretary Henry Paulson's and Federal Reserve Board chairman Ben Bernanke's insistence six weeks earlier that there was no time for Congress to think, only time for it to act on a financial sector bailout (i.e., TARP [Troubled Asset Relief Program]), lest the economy face financial ruin.

About the economic situation at that time, incoming White House chief of staff Rahm Emanuel said, "You never want a serious crisis to go to waste ... [t]his crisis provides the opportunity for us to do things that you could not do before."

The mainstream media obliged the script, elevating the automobile industry "crisis" to the top of the news cycle for the next month, and helping to characterize the debate in the simplistic, polarizing dichotomy of "Main Street versus Wall Street." The notion that some financial institutions took risks, lost big, and were rescued by Washington became the prevailing argument for bailing out the auto companies, and the specific facts about viability and worthiness were all but totally ignored.

But public opinion quickly changed when the CEOs [chief executive officers] of GM, Ford, and Chrysler laid waste to months of public relations planning and millions of dollars spent trying to cultivate a winning message when they each arrived in Washington, tin cups in hand, aboard their own corporate jets. That fateful episode turned the media against Detroit and reminded Americans—or at least opened their minds to the prospect—that the automakers were in dire straits because of bad decisions made in the past and helped convince many that a shake out, instead of a bailout, was the proper course of action. A few weeks later, on the same day that the CEOs returned to Washington, attempting to show contrition by making the trip from Detroit in their companies' most eco-friendly cars, a new automobile assembly plant opened for business in Greensburg, Indiana. Although the hearing on Capitol Hill received far more media coverage, the unveiling of Honda's newest facility in the American heartland spoke volumes about the true state of the U.S. car industry— and provided another example of why the bailout was misguided. The U.S. auto industry was not at risk. Two companies were suffering the consequences of years of incompetence and inefficiency exacerbated by persistent overcapacity and a deep recession. Normal bankruptcies for the two automakers were viable options, but certain stakeholders didn't like their prospects under those circumstances.

Today, when President Obama contends that his administration saved the auto industry, he evokes memories of those CAR projections of 2–3 million job losses in the absence of government intervention. Without those inflated figures concocted during a time of "crisis," the 225,000 jobs lost in the auto sector since November 2008 seem quite mild—even worthy of praise.

That Which Is Seen

While bailout enthusiasts hail GM's first-quarter earnings as proof that the administration saved the auto industry, President Obama should know better than to gloat. No such feat was accomplished and the imperative of extricating the government from GM's operations has yet to be achieved.

With profits of $3.2 billion, the first quarter of 2011 was GM's best performance in ten years and its fifth-consecutive profitable quarter. That's good for GM, and predictably those earnings have been hailed by some as a validation of government intervention. The *Washington Post*'s E.J. Dionne asserted: "Far too little attention has been paid to the success of the government's rescue of the Detroit-based auto companies, and almost no attention has been paid to how completely and utterly wrong opponents of the bailout were when they insisted it was doomed to failure."

Former Michigan governor Jennifer Granholm tweeted: "To all of you in the strangle-government crowd, who said the bailout would never work—I'm just sayin."

Dionne and Granholm have created a straw man, contending that bailout critics thought that the government couldn't resuscitate GM. But the most thoughtful criticism of the bailout was not predicated on the notion that GM couldn't be saved by the government marshaling the vast resources at its disposal. That opposition was borne of concern that the government would do just that, and in the process impose many more costs and inflict greater damage. And that's what it did.

But Dionne and Granholm, like others before them, stand slack-jawed, in awe, ready and willing to buy the Brooklyn Bridge, donning blinders and viewing just a narrow sliver of the world, oblivious to the fact that related events have been transpiring in the other 359 degrees that surround him. . . .

But only the most gullible observers would accept GM's profits as an appropriate measure of the wisdom of the auto bailout. Those profits speak only to the fact that politicians committed over $50 billion to the task of rescuing a single company. With debts expunged, cash infused, inefficiencies severed, ownership reconstituted, sales rebates underwritten, and political obstacles steamrolled—all in the midst of a cyclical U.S. recovery and structural global expansion in auto demand—only the most incompetent operation could fail to make big profits. To that point, it's worth noting that more than half of GM's reported profit—$1.8 billion of $3.2 billion—is attributable to the onetime sales of shares in Ally Financial and Delphi, which says nothing about whether GM can make and sell automobiles profitably going forward.

In the process of "rescuing" GM, the government opened a Pandora's box. Any legitimate verdict on the efficacy of the intervention must account for the costs of mitigating the problems that escaped the box.

Spoils of Competition Denied—Market Process Short-Circuited

The intervention on GM's behalf denied the spoils of competition—the market share, sales revenues, profits, and productive assets—to Ford, Honda, Hyundai, and all of the other automakers that made better products, made better operational decisions, were more efficient, or were more responsive to consumer demands than GM, thereby short-circuiting a feedback loop that is essential to the healthy functioning of competitive market economies.

Corporate bailouts are clearly unfair to taxpayers, but they are also unfair to the successful firms in the industry, who are implicitly taxed and burdened when their competition is subsidized. In a properly functioning market economy, the better firms—the ones that are more innovative, more efficient, and more popular among consumers—gain market share or increase profits, while the lesser firms contract. This process ensures that limited resources are used most productively.

It has been suggested that I view GM's fate as a matter of national indifference. That's correct, because I have not made the mistake of conflating GM's condition with that of the U.S. auto industry. Whether or not there are so-called "national interests" in ensuring the existence of a healthy domestic auto industry (and I'm not convinced there are), health comes through an evolutionary process in which the companies that have made the right decisions survive and grow, and those that have made bad decisions contract and sometimes even disappear.

It is not only fair, but efficient and wise that the market rewards companies that make better products at better prices with higher profits and larger market shares, while the companies that make undesirable products at high cost lose profits and market share.

There is still enormous overcapacity in the U.S. auto industry, reconciliation of which the bailout of GM (and Chrysler) has deferred at great cost to the other firms and their workers.

Weakening of the Rule of Law

Although legislation to provide funding for an auto bailout passed in the House of Representatives in December 2008, the bill did not garner enough support in the Senate, where it died. Prospects for any form of taxpayer bailout seemed remote and the proper course of action for GM and Chrysler, reorganization under Chapter 11, appeared imminent. An interventionist bullet, seemingly, had been dodged.

But then, just days after then secretary Paulson claimed to have no authority to use TARP funds to support the auto companies, President [George W.] Bush announced that he would authorize bridge loans from the TARP of $17.4 billion to GM and Chrysler. That opened the door to further mischief and, ultimately, another $60 billion was diverted from TARP by the Obama administration for unauthorized purposes related to the auto bailout. Likewise, the Obama administration treated the GM (and Chrysler) bankruptcy as a Section 363 sale, which are known among bankruptcy lawyers as "Sham" sales. These 363 sales are intended to sell assets out of bankruptcy from one company to another, but are not intended as vehicles to facilitate entire corporate restructurings. In a reorganization process, all creditors are given the right to vote on the proposed plan, as well as the opportunity to offer competing reorganization plans. A 363 asset sale has no such requirements, and is being used increasingly by companies seeking to avert paying legitimate claims to creditors.

That the U.S. executive branch would pretend that the restructuring of GM was nothing more than an asset sale and deny creditors the right to vote or to offer competing bids wreaks of crony capitalism.

Though it is a difficult cost to quantify, executive branch overreach—to put it mildly—is a threat to the U.S. system of checks and balances and an affront to the rule of law.

Executive Encroachment into Bankruptcy Process

General Motors was a perfectly viable company that could have been restructured through normal bankruptcy proceedings. The big question was whether GM could have received financing to operate during bankruptcy, given the problems in credit markets in 2008 and 2009. Instead of commandeering the bankruptcy process as a condition of providing debtor in possession financing, the Obama administration could have provided the funds and allowed an apolitical, independent bankruptcy process to take place. But the administration's rationale for a hands-on approach was that it wanted to ensure that taxpayers weren't just throwing good money after bad, chasing empty promises made by executives with credibility problems. Yet, even with the administration's plans for GM's post-bankruptcy ownership thrust upon the company without allowance for consideration of competing plans, taxpayers will lose between $10–20 billion (without considering the $12 to $14 billion costs of the unorthodox tax breaks granted GM by the administration).

The administration's willingness to insulate important political allies, like the UAW [International Union, United Automobile, Aerospace and Agricultural Implement Workers of America, commonly known as United Automobile Workers], from the consequences of their decisions, to shift possession

The Car Companies Ask for a Bailout

As bad as the Senate hearing was, the next day was worse. As the House Financial Services Committee's hearing was concluding, an ABC News reporter buttonholed [General Motors Company chief executive officer (CEO) Rick] Wagoner and [Ford Motor Company CEO Alan Roger] Mulally at the witness table to ask a question. How could they plead poverty, he wanted to know, when they had flown to Washington on their luxury corporate jets?

The CEOs bolted like a Corvette peeling away from a stoplight, which only made the damage worse when their hasty retreats were replayed on the evening news. ABC reported that the corporate jet flights had cost the companies $20,000 each, compared to the price of $200 for a commercial airline ticket.

The congressmen, predictably, pounced. "There's a delicious irony in seeing private luxury jets flying into Washington and people coming off them with tin cups in their hands," snapped one Democrat. "It's like seeing a guy show up at the soup kitchen in high hat and tuxedo."

Paul Ingrassia, Crash Course: The American Automobile Industry's Road to Bankruptcy and Bailout—and Beyond. *New York: Random House, 2010, pp. 219–220.*

of assets from shareholders and debt holders to pensioners, and to deny "deficiency" claims to creditors who were short-changed, will make it more difficult for companies in politically important industries to borrow from private sources when they are in trouble, thereby increasing their reliance on the government purse.

The government's willingness to intervene in the auto market under false pretenses to pick winners and losers is a significant cause of the regime uncertainty that has pervaded the U.S. economy, deterred business investment and job creation, and slowed the economic recovery ever since.

Outstanding Financial Costs

As Washington has been embroiled in a discussion about national finances that features figures in the trillions of dollars, one might be tempted to marginalize as paltry the sum still owed taxpayers from the GM bailout. That figure is estimated to be about $27 billion, which accounts for the $50 billion outlay minus approximately $23 billion raised at GM's IPO [initial public offering] last November. But that is a very conservative figure considering that it excludes $12–$14 billion in unorthodox tax breaks granted to GM in bankruptucy; $17 billion in funds committed from TARP to GM's former financial arm GMAC (which was supported to facilitate GM sales); GM's portion of the $25 billion Energy Department slush fund to underwrite research and development in green auto technology; and the $7,500 tax credit granted for every new purchase of a Chevy Volt [a plug-in hybrid electric vehicle]. There may be other subsidies, as well.

With respect to GM, taxpayers are on the line for much more than is commonly discussed.

The administration wants to put maximum distance between the episode of GM's nationalization and the 2012 campaign season, which is nearly upon us. In that regard, the administration would like to sell the Treasury's remaining 500 million shares as soon as possible. But the administration would also like to "make the taxpayers whole." The problem for the president on that score is that the stock price—even with all of the happy news about the auto industry turnaround—isn't cooperating. As of this morning [June 22, 2011], GM stock is hovering just under $30 per share. If all of the 500 million remaining publicly owned shares could be sold at that price, the Treasury would net $15 billion. Add that to the $23 billion raised from the initial public offering last November, and the "direct" public loss on GM is about $12 billion—calculated as a $50 billion outlay minus a $38 billion return. (And not considering all of the extra costs identified above.)

To net $50 billion, those 500 million public shares must be sold at an average price of just over $53—a virtual impossibility anytime soon. Why? The most significant factor suppressing the stock value is the market's knowledge that the largest single holder of GM stock wants to unload about 500 million shares in the short term. That fact will continue to trump any positive news about GM and its profit potential, not that such news should be expected.

Projections about gasoline prices vary, but as long as prices at the pump remain in the $4 range, GM is going to suffer. Among major automakers, GM is most exposed to the downside of high gasoline prices. Despite all of the subsidies and all of the hoopla over the Chevy Volt (only 1,700 units have been sold through April 2011) and the Chevy Cruze (now subject to a steering column recall that won't help repair negative quality perceptions), GM does not have much of a competitive presence in the small car market. Though GM held the largest overall U.S. market share in 2010, it had the smallest share (8.4%) of the small car market, which is where the demand will be if high gas prices persist. GM will certainly have to do better in that segment once the federally mandated average fleet fuel-efficiency standard rises to 35.5 miles per gallon in 2016.

Reaping what it sowed, the administration finds itself in an unenviable position. It can entirely divest of GM in the short term at what would likely be a $10-to-$20 billion taxpayer loss (the stock price will drop if 500 million shares are put up for sale in short period) and face the ire of an increasingly cost- and budget-conscious electorate. Or the adminis- tration can hold on to the stock, hoping against hope that GM experiences economic fortunes good enough to more than compensate for the stock price–suppressing effect of the market's knowledge of an imminent massive sales, while con- tending with accusations of market meddling and industrial policy.

The longer the administration retains shares in GM, it will be tempted to meddle to achieve politically desirable results.

Redefining Success

Or, the administration can do what it is going to do: First, lower expectations that the taxpayer will ever recover $50 bil- lion. Here's a recent statement by Tim Geithner: "We're going to lose money in the auto industry. . . . We didn't do these things to maximize return. We did them to save jobs. The big- gest impact of these programs was in the millions of jobs saved." That's a safe counterfactual, since it can never be tested or proved. (There are 225,000 fewer jobs in the auto industry as of April 2011 than there were in November 2008, when the bailout process began.)

Second, the administration will argue that the Obama ad- ministration is only on the hook for $40 billion (the first $10 billion having come from Bush). In a post-IPO November 2010 statement revealing of a man less concerned with the nation's finances than his own political prospects, President Obama asserted: "American taxpayers are now positioned to recover more than *my administration* invested in GM, and that's a good thing." (My emphasis).

Lasting Implications

The lasting implications of the bailout will depend on whether or not Americans ultimately accept the narrative that the bail- out was a success. If it is considered a success, the threshold for interventions will have been lowered and Americans will have the opportunity to judge similar bailouts in the future. If it is considered a failure—as it should be—the lasting implications will be less destructive because the threshold that tempts interventionists will be higher. On that score, contrary to what the administration would have the public believe, gauging the "success" of the GM bailout requires consideration of more than just the ratio of finances recouped over financial outlays.

There are numerous other costs that don't factor into that equation. If the bailout is considered a success, some of the likely lasting implications will include the following:

- Fearmongering will be considered an effective technique to stifle debate and enable a stampede toward the politically expedient outcome

- Americans will be more willing to extend powers without serious objection to the executive branch that we would not extend in the absence of a perceived crisis

- An increase in government interventions and bailouts of politically important entities

- Greater diversion of productive assets (resources for R&D [research and development] and engineering) to political ends (lobbying and lawyering)

- A greater uncertainty to the business climate, as the rule of law is weakened and higher risk premiums are assigned to U.S. economic activity

- Riskier behavior from Ford Motor Company, knowing it has "banked" its bailout

- A greater push from the administration for a comprehensive national industrial policy

- Less aversion to subsidization of chosen industries abroad

Bad Consequences

The objection to the auto bailout was not that the federal government wouldn't be able to marshal adequate resources to help GM. The most serious concerns were about the consequences of that intervention—the undermining of the rule of law, the property confiscations, the politically driven decisions and the distortion of market signals.

Any verdict on the auto bailouts must take into account, among other things, the illegal diversion of TARP funds; the forced transfer of assets from shareholders and debt holders to pensioners and their union; the higher-risk premiums consequently built into U.S. corporate debt; the costs of denying Ford and the other more worthy automakers the spoils of competition; the costs of insulating irresponsible actors, such as the autoworkers' union, from the outcomes of an apolitical bankruptcy proceeding; the diminution of U.S. moral authority to counsel foreign governments against market interventions; and the lingering uncertainty about policy that pervades the business environment to this day.

GM's recent profits speak only to the fact that politicians committed more than $50 billion to the task of rescuing those companies and the United Automobile Workers. With debts expunged, cash infused, inefficiencies severed, ownership reconstituted, sales rebates underwritten and political obstacles steamrolled—all in the midst of a recovery in U.S. auto demand—only the most incompetent operations could fail to make profits.

But taxpayers are still short at least $10 billion to $20 billion (depending on the price that the government's 500 million shares of GM will fetch), and there is still significant overcapacity in the auto industry.

The administration should divest as soon as possible, without regard to the stock price. Keeping the government's tentacles around a large firm in an important industry will keep the door open wider to industrial policy and will deter market-driven decision making throughout the industry, possibly keeping the brakes on the recovery. Yes, there will be a significant loss to taxpayers. But the right lesson to learn from this chapter in history is that government interventions carry real economic costs—only some of which are readily measurable.

| "It was the most successful peacetime
industrial intervention in U.S. history."

In Michigan, Will Romney Regret Opposing Auto Bailout?

Andy Sullivan

Andy Sullivan is a journalist at Reuters. In the following viewpoint, he reports that 2012 Republican presidential candidate Mitt Romney did not want the government to bail out the auto industry in 2008. Sullivan says, at the time, that this may hurt Romney in the 2012 election in Michigan. Romney, Sullivan says, continues to claim that normal bankruptcy, without bailout, would have been effective. However, Sullivan reports, experts have argued that the financial crisis and banks' reluctance to lend money would have made a normal bankruptcy for the auto industry impossible. Sullivan says that the success of the bailout may help Barack Obama in Michigan in the election.

As you read, consider the following questions:

1. How was Romney's father connected to the auto industry, according to the viewpoint?

2. According to Sullivan, what did the Obama administration do with regard to General Motors Company (GM) and Chrysler Group during the bailout?

3. According to Romney's spokesperson, how did events prove Romney right about the bailout?

Four years ago [in 2008], Republican presidential candidate Mitt Romney stood at the gates of a Michigan factory and vowed to fight for the U.S. auto industry as it slid toward collapse.

Romney and the Bailout

Now, with Romney desperate for a win in Michigan's primary on February 28 [2012], he will have to explain to voters why later in 2008, he called for the U.S. government to stand aside as auto companies at the brink of insolvency begged for help.

Romney, the son of a former auto executive and Michigan governor, opposed an $81 billion government bailout that ensured the survival of General Motors [Company] and Chrysler [Group] and that some industry experts say saved 1.3 million jobs.

The former private equity executive, who built a fortune in part by overhauling struggling businesses, has argued that the auto industry would have recovered on its own.

The industry's unlikely rebound has been a rare feel-good story in Michigan, which is struggling to emerge from the 2007–2009 recession. It has inspired Super Bowl TV ads linking the industry's turnaround with national pride, and given Democratic president Barack Obama a success story to tout as evidence that his recession-fighting efforts are paying off.

But for Romney, who in 2008 wrote a *New York Times* opinion piece titled "Let Detroit Go Bankrupt," the industry's comeback poses a delicate political question: Whether he can defend his stance on the bailout while deflecting familiar accusations he flip-flops on issues and has little empathy for the struggles of working Americans.

"It's just going to be hard for him to explain, and yet he's going to have to continue to make that case or come up with some new answer," said Bill Ballenger, editor of the *Inside Michigan Politics* newsletter.

Romney's anti-bailout stance is unlikely to keep him from winning conservatives' support in Michigan's Republican primary, political analysts say. Recent polls show him leading the race by 5 to 15 percentage points, and he won the primary in 2008 during his unsuccessful run for the Republican nomination.

But if he goes on to win the Republican nomination, his stance could be a liability in a matchup against Obama this autumn, when Michigan will be an important battleground, political analysts say.

Obama Touts Success

Romney's Republican rivals Newt Gingrich, Rick Santorum and Ron Paul also opposed the auto bailout, but none has spoken so extensively on the topic.

Romney's father, George Romney, ran American Motors [Corporation] in the 1950s and 1960s before serving as Michigan governor. Mitt Romney announced his 2008 presidential bid in Michigan, on a stage flanked by Detroit-made cars.

During that campaign, Romney called for quadrupling federal spending on energy and automotive research, to $20 billion a year.

He criticized Senator John McCain, the eventual Republican nominee, for suggesting that some lost manufacturing jobs would not return to Michigan.

"The auto industry and all its jobs do not have to be lost. And I am one man who will work to transform the industry and save those jobs," Romney said at the Detroit Economic Club on January 14, 2008.

But in November of that year, Romney argued for a hands-off approach as Republican president George W. Bush weighed emergency loans for GM, Chrysler and Ford [Motor Company].

Romney argued in the *Times* article that the automakers should not get government help but instead go through a private bankruptcy process to trim costs.

That is not what happened.

The U.S. government, first under Bush and then under Obama, committed $49.5 billion in working capital and loans to GM and $12.5 billion to Chrysler. Nearly $20 billion more in related financing went to suppliers, dealers and auto-financing firms.

The Obama administration pushed the bailed-out automakers into bankruptcy in early 2009, taking ownership of GM and forcing Chrysler into a merger with Italy's Fiat S.p.A.

The bailout led to tens of thousands of job cuts and ultimately could cost the government $20 billion. But it allowed the companies to become profitable at lower sales volumes by revamping labor contracts and reducing capacity.

GM regained its title as the world's top-selling automaker last month. Chrysler recently told workers they would get a bonus based on the company's strong performance.

Michigan's bartered economy has begun to show signs of improvement. The state's unemployment rate fell from 14.1 percent in August 2009 to 9.8 percent in November 2011— still well above the national average.

Obama and top administration officials have made frequent trips to Michigan to tout the revitalization, arguably their top economic accomplishment.

"It's good to remember the fact that there were some folks who were willing to let this industry die," Obama said last week, in an apparent jab at Romney.

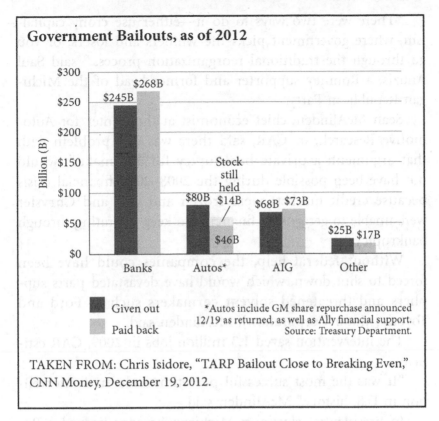

Government Bailouts, as of 2012

Billion (B)

- $300 — $268B
- $245B
- $250
- $200
- $150 — Stock still held
- $100 — $80B $14B $68B $73B
- $50 — $46B $25B $17B
- $0

Banks   Autos*   AIG   Other

■ Given out
■ Paid back

*Autos include GM share repurchase announced 12/19 as returned, as well as Ally financial support.
Source: Treasury Department.

TAKEN FROM: Chris Isidore, "TARP Bailout Close to Breaking Even," CNN Money, December 19, 2012.

The Romney campaign has stuck to its guns, arguing that the administration would have saved billions of dollars if it had followed Romney's advice.

"Events have proved Governor Romney exactly right," campaign spokeswoman Amanda Henneberg said. "It is unfortunate that the government first attempted a bailout, which was precisely as unsuccessful as he predicted, cost taxpayers billions, and left the government improperly entangled in the private sector."

Debating the Government's Role

Romney supporters point out that airlines and other large businesses have been able to reorganize in bankruptcy without government help.

"There were two ways to do it—either use crony capitalism, where government picks the winners and losers, or you go through the traditional reorganization process," said Saul Anuzis, a Romney supporter and former head of the Michigan Republican Party.

Sean McAlinden, chief economist at the Center for Automotive Research, or CAR, said there was one problem with that argument: a private bankruptcy for automakers would not have been possible during the 2008–2009 financial crisis because credit markets were frozen and GM and Chrysler were unable to get private financing to keep operating through bankruptcy.

Without federal help, the companies could have been forced to shut down, which would have devastated parts suppliers and threatened solvent carmakers such as Ford and Toyota [Motor Corporation], McAlinden said.

The intervention saved 1.3 million jobs in 2009, CAR estimates.

"It was the most successful peacetime industrial intervention in U.S. history," McAlinden said.

In presidential elections, Michigan has not backed a Republican candidate since 1988. Obama won the state by 16 points in 2008. The state is widely seen as a toss-up this fall because of the battering it took during the recession.

The bailout could give Obama an edge in November.

The president's job approval rating averaged 48 percent in Michigan in 2011, according to Gallup—his best showing among the 13 "swing" states widely projected to be especially competitive this fall.

"I would think Obama gets his fair share of credit, and that would be among all voters—Democrat, Republican and independent," said Craig Ruff, a senior policy fellow at Public Sector Consultants, a nonpartisan Michigan think tank.

"He won't have an easy time carrying Michigan ... but it's certainly a leg up for him."

> *"The creditors got a pretty decent recovery given the circumstances, and the world didn't come to an end."*

Lehman Recovery Seen as Justifying $2 Billion Bankruptcy

Erik Larson

Erik Larson is a Bloomberg legal reporter. In the following viewpoint, he reports on the outcome of the Lehman Brothers Holdings Inc. bankruptcy. Lehman, a global financial services firm, collapsed in 2008, sparking a worldwide financial collapse. The US government refused to bail out Lehman, which pushed the company into bankruptcy. Larson reports that the result of that bankruptcy overall has been a success. Creditors have received some return on their investments, and the company is moving forward. The worst fears about the world economy were not realized, though there was a dangerous and costly recession.

As you read, consider the following questions:

1. What does Robert Lawless say about Lehman's fees for legal services in bankruptcy?

2. What does Larson say Ben Bernanke and Henry Paulson got wrong about the Lehman bankruptcy?

3. Under what circumstances does Larson say fees and expenses for Lehman's bankruptcy could have been lower?

Harvey Miller, the lawyer guiding Lehman Brothers Holdings Inc. through the biggest-ever U.S. bankruptcy, sipped a cappuccino at a tourist-filled cafe near Manhattan's Central Park and reflected on how his client's collapse five years ago [in 2008] went from unthinkable to inevitable.

Lehman's demise "ignited a worldwide conflagration that almost brought down the global financial system," said Miller, who filed the Chapter 11 petition at 2 a.m. on Sept. 15, 2008, in New York after the bank failed to win U.S. government aid or attract a buyer. "The consequences were unknown."

Five years later, Miller takes credit for helping fend off some creditors' liquidation demands and instead turning the remains of one of the biggest failures of the financial crisis into a going concern [referring to a business that functions without the threat of liquidation for the foreseeable future]. In the process, the Lehman estate has paid more than $2 billion in fees and expenses to professionals like him for that work, dwarfing the previous record of $757 million in Enron Corp.'s bankruptcy.

In exchange for that eye-popping payday, approved by the judge in charge of the case, Lehman creditors are poised to get 18 cents on the dollar by 2016, from an estate valued at $65 billion, according to a liquidation plan approved in December 2011. Miller, 80, estimated that recovery may rise to as much as 22 cents as the value of Lehman's assets increases over the next three years to about $80 billion.

His estimate is a "somewhat educated guess," Miller said in an interview near the offices of his law firm, New York–based Weil, Gotshal & Manges LLP. "I am sure debt traders have their own projected recovery valuations."

$43 Billion

Lehman, which listed $613 billion in debt when it filed, is scheduled to pay out $14 billion to creditors on Oct. 3, bringing total distributions to $43 billion since the Chapter 11 plan was approved, according to court records and Miller.

Miller's firm, which also worked on the Enron case, has made almost $500 million since the Lehman bankruptcy started, and more than $600 million has gone to the restructuring company Alvarez & Marsal Inc., whose employees ran Lehman after the collapse and are still unwinding complex derivatives contracts to generate cash for creditors.

The Lehman case is "one of a kind" and should be viewed as a success, even with the fees, said Stephen Lubben, a bankruptcy professor at Seton Hall University School of Law in Newark, New Jersey.

"The creditors got a pretty decent recovery given the circumstances, and the world didn't come to an end," Lubben said in a phone interview. "If you think of the fees as the price the creditors pay to get this recovery, I'm sure most of them would be willing to pay."

Historical Norms

Robert Lawless, a professor at the University of Illinois College of Law in Champaign, said Lehman's fees are well within historical norms for very large cases, particularly for a case involving assets of $639 billion. He said fees usually total 2 percent to 4 percent of a bankrupt company's assets.

"It's easy to be outraged and say it shouldn't happen, but is this emblematic of a system that's broken and isn't working? I can't look at $2 billion in fees in a $639 billion case and say that," Lawless said in a phone interview.

Miller said the fees are reasonable considering they went to hundreds of people, including financial advisers, investment bankers, forensic accountants, appraisers, tax specialists, real estate specialists and regulatory specialists.

"It has been the largest, most complex case ever filed," he said in an e-mail. "Professionals had to be engaged all over the world to protect Lehman assets."

The judge-approved expenses would have been higher if not for cuts sought by Tracy Hope Davis, the U.S. trustee who supervises bankruptcies for the Justice Department. Davis has objected repeatedly to payments that she argued were "not reasonable." She has also criticized creditors such as Goldman Sachs Group Inc. that fought Lehman to improve their own payout and then asked the estate to pay their lawyers.

Big Cases

Another reason Weil and other bankruptcy lawyers might have received the stamp of approval for most of their proposed fees: Judges don't often challenge payments to attorneys whose firms bring in big cases because those lawyers are free to take future filings to competing courts that won't question the fees, Lynn LoPucki, a bankruptcy professor at the University of California, Los Angeles, said in his 2005 book *Courting Failure: How Competition for Big Cases Is Corrupting the Bankruptcy Courts.*

Alvarez & Marsal chief executive officer Bryan Marsal, who led Lehman after the bankruptcy, said in 2009 that it made more sense to stretch out the process and incur more fees because it was smarter to manage the bank's properties to maximize their value rather than liquidate them at "fire sale" prices.

Miller said that plan worked. Marsal, 62, had no immediate comment on the case.

Lehman technically exited bankruptcy in March 2012, although the case will linger for three to five more years as the reorganization is executed and related multibillion-dollar lawsuits are dealt with, Miller said.

"Humongous Failure"

"We were dealing with a humongous failure and we achieved a realization of value that was unanticipated," according to Miller, who wouldn't say how much he was personally paid for the case. "Almost everybody has been surprised by the success of the administration."

Miller, who also worked on the General Motors bankruptcy, said the expense can be blamed in part on the Lehman case's chaotic start, after Federal Reserve chairman Ben Bernanke and then U.S. treasury secretary [Henry] Paulson declined to bail out the 158-year-old firm.

The pair wrongly concluded that any disruption from the collapse of the world's fourth-biggest investment bank would stabilize within a few days and that it should therefore be allowed to die, Miller said.

"Bernanke and Paulson were under the impression that the financial markets were prepared for Lehman's demise," he said. "They were wrong. They were so wrong that the financial markets almost collapsed."

White House

Paulson said at a White House briefing on the day of the bankruptcy that he "never once considered it appropriate to put taxpayer money on the line in resolving Lehman Brothers." That decision contrasted with deals he helped broker to provide Fed financing for JPMorgan Chase & Co. (JPM)'s agreement in March that year to buy Bear Stearns Cos. and his takeover of mortgage-finance companies Freddie Mac [Federal Home Loan Mortgage Corporation] and Fannie Mae [Federal National Mortgage Association].

Miller's highest-profile success for Lehman came early on when the company's still-functioning brokerage unit was sold to Barclays Plc (BARC) for $1.75 billion—a figure based mostly on the value of Lehman's headquarters in Manhattan and two data centers in New Jersey. The court approved the

The History of Lehman Brothers

In 2008, Lehman Brothers [Holding Inc.], the fourth-largest investment bank in the United State, filed for Chapter 11 bankruptcy.

Lehman Brothers was founded by Henry, Emanuel, and Mayer Lehman, German immigrants who migrated to America in the mid-nineteenth century. It opened its first store in Montgomery, Alabama, in 1850. As cotton was the cash crop of the South, the brothers often accepted payment in cotton and began acting as brokers for those who were buying and selling the crop. The brothers' business expanded quickly, and they opened an office in New York in 1858. Soon they had transformed from brokerage to merchant banking, and Lehman Brothers became a member of the New York Stock Exchange in 1887.

The company continued to thrive even through the stock market crash of 1929. . . . In 2007, the year the subprime crisis began, Lehman Brothers was ranked as number one in the "Most Admired Firms" list by *Fortune* magazine. . . . For its third quarter, Lehman Brothers possessed assets worth $275 billion.

Then the subprime mortgage crisis came to a head. By late 2008, the company's shares had lost 73 percent of their value. . . . The company filed for bankruptcy that year, with $613 billion in debt. . . . The bank received some relief after Barclays PLC agreed to purchase much of Lehman Brothers for $1.75 billion. . . . Yet this did little to help many shareholders, who had already seen their stocks reduced to nothing.

O.C. Ferrell, John Fraedrich, and Linda Ferrell,
Business Ethics: Ethical Decision Making and Cases. *8th ed.*
Stamford, CT: Cengage Learning, 2011.

sale at a speed that U.S. bankruptcy judge James Peck in Manhattan said at the time was "unheard of."

Archstone Sale

More recently, in November, Lehman agreed to sell its Archstone Inc. (ARS) apartment unit to Sam Zell's Equity Residential (EQR) and AvalonBay Communities Inc. (AVB) for $6.5 billion, dropping plans to take the company public in an initial stock offering. The price included $2.69 billion in cash along with stock valued at $3.8 billion.

The fees and expenses could have been lower if Lehman had had more time to prepare the filing and create a plan in advance, said Chip Bowles, a bankruptcy lawyer at Bingham Greenebaum Doll LLP in Louisville, Kentucky.

The case was "so complex, so nasty, so heavily litigated, it's very hard to come back and say you could have saved money here and there," he said. "Bankruptcies, when they are planned and organized, are cheaper than those that are chaotic."

In June, three months after Lehman's plan took effect, Weil fired 60 salaried attorneys and 110 staff and cut some partners' pay. Miller said such developments are predictable when a big case like Lehman winds down.

Claims Basis

He also said there's no basis for claims that Lehman took too long to begin repaying creditors.

"Other big cases have taken much longer," he said. "Given the complexity and size of the case, it's extraordinary that distribution has occurred in only four and a half years."

The fees are justified given the effort put into the case, including many days of "24-7" work by employees, Miller said. He compared attorneys' compensation to that of plumbers, who are also paid by the hour, "though plumbers are more appreciated than lawyers."

Weil, which represented Lehman in financial matters for more than two decades before the bankruptcy, won court approval in 2008 to bill as much as $950 an hour for its top lawyers. That figure rose to $990 by 2010 and as much as $1,000 for partners working overseas, court records show.

"When you're working on an hourly basis, it's not a great way to make money," Miller said. "If you come up with a good idea that's very valuable, you only get paid one hour for it."

"*The trigger for the financial crisis, in other words, could have been the market's loss of confidence in a solvent firm.*"

The Government Should Have Bailed Lehman Out of Bankruptcy

Peter J. Wallison

Peter J. Wallison is the Arthur F. Burns Fellow in Financial Policy Studies at the American Enterprise Institute. He was a member of the Financial Crisis Inquiry Commission of the US government. In the following viewpoint, he argues that the Federal Reserve's reasons for not bailing out financial services company Lehman Brothers Holdings Inc. do not make sense in retrospect. Lehman Brothers was better off than the Federal Reserve claimed, Wallison says, and therefore bailing the company out would have been feasible. Wallison concludes that the financial panic in 2008 was caused not by real financial disaster but by poor decisions by the Federal Reserve that ended up panicking the market.

Peter J. Wallison, "The Fed vs. the FDIC on Lehman's Failure," *American*, April 27, 2011.

As you read, consider the following questions:

1. Why did the Federal Reserve initially say it could not bail out Lehman Brothers, according to Wallison?

2. What does Wallison say the financial markets assumed after the Federal Reserve bailed out Bear Stearns?

3. How much does Wallison say Lehman Brothers' creditors would have lost through liquidation, and why does he see this as significant?

As we all know, the 2008 financial crisis began in earnest when [financial services company] Lehman Brothers [Holdings Inc.] filed for bankruptcy. It has always been a question why Lehman was allowed to fail when Bear Stearns [Companies]—a smaller firm—was rescued with $30 billion of Federal Reserve [Fed] financial support to JPMorgan Chase. Questions were even more pointed when the Fed rescued AIG [American International Group Inc.] only days after it let Lehman descend into bankruptcy. Now the U.S. Federal Deposit Insurance Corporation (FDIC) has shed its own light on the issue. In a report last week [in April 2011], the FDIC claimed that the losses would have been far smaller than initially estimated if Lehman Brothers had received government financial support to avert its bankruptcy and eventually been wound down or sold.

Questionable Decisions

After the calamitous market reaction to Lehman's failure in September 2008, the Treasury Department and the Fed initially argued that the Fed did not have the legal authority to rescue Lehman. This turned out to be a bit of obfuscation when a Fed lawyer testified to the Financial Crisis Inquiry Commission [FCIC] that it was only necessary for the Fed's board of governors to have adopted an appropriate resolution. In his testimony to the FCIC, Fed chairman Ben Bernanke did

not dispute this fact, but said it would not have been responsible to rescue Lehman because it was so far underwater that
the Fed would simply have been throwing good money after
bad. "There was not nearly enough collateral to provide
enough liquidity to meet the run [on Lehman]. The company
would fail anyway, and the Federal Reserve would be left holding this very illiquid collateral, a very large amount of it." In
other words, the Fed did not save Lehman the way it saved
Bear because Lehman simply did not have enough available
collateral to protect the Fed against losses if it attempted, with
liquidity support, to stop the run.

In its new report, however, the FDIC claims that if it had
been able to use the resolution powers later granted under the
Dodd-Frank Act [the Dodd-Frank Wall Street Reform and
Consumer Protection Act], losses to Lehman's creditors would
have been limited to three cents on the dollar—far less than
the losses Bernanke had suggested. Given the uncertainties as-
sociated with the facts of the Lehman case and the FDIC's
own inexperience with resolving nonbank financial institutions, one should take this estimate with a large grain of salt.

Still, if it is anywhere close to reality, the FDIC's conten-
tion that Lehman's creditors would have lost only three cents
on the dollar again calls into question the U.S. government's
decision to let Lehman fail. Clearly, after Bear Stearns's rescue,
the financial markets were assuming that the United States
would rescue all larger firms. This was confirmed by Anton
Valukas's report as an examiner for the U.S. bankruptcy court.
Most market participants, he reported, including Lehman,
could not imagine why the Fed would rescue Bear Stearns and
not Lehman. When Lehman was allowed to fail, market participants realized that they did not know who would survive
and who would not. A massive panic ensued as financial institutions hoarded cash.

Indeed, in the Valukas and FDIC accounts, Lehman does
not look like the basket case Bernanke portrayed. According to

the Valukas report, Lehman had raised at least $10 billion dollars in additional capital in April and June 2008, and the FDIC noted that in September 2008—the month Lehman filed for bankruptcy—the firm had equity and subordinated debt of $35 billion. It also had $50 to $70 billion in impaired assets of questionable value, most of which had been identified by the diligence examinations of various suitors. Assuming a loss ratio of 60 to 80 percent on these assets, the FDIC estimated that Lehman in liquidation would have lost about $5 billion.

Policy Failures

The difference between the FDIC and the Fed about the financial condition of Lehman before its failure is no small matter. It not only puts in doubt the Fed's account of its decision making, but it also raises significant questions about the nature of the financial crisis. If Lehman's creditors would have lost only 3 percent in a liquidation, the firm might actually have been solvent as a going concern [a business that functions without the threat of liquidation for the foreseeable future]. As difficult as it is to imagine, the trigger for the financial crisis, in other words, could have been the market's loss of confidence in a solvent firm.

The financial crisis was triggered by the meltdown of the U.S. housing bubble, which in turn caused the collapse of the market for mortgage-backed securities. With that market gone, mark-to-market accounting required the write-down of asset values on the balance sheets of financial institutions around the world. In many cases, these losses turned out to be temporary accounting losses. U.S. banks today are adding back into their earnings the heavy provisions that they had made for losses on mortgage-backed securities. Was the financial crisis, then, a recognition of real losses and weaknesses in the financial system—as initially portrayed—or only a world-class panic induced by investor uncertainty about the scope of housing losses, made worse by a series of major policy-maker errors?

> "AIG was in many ways the 'good' bail-
> out, where shareholders were almost
> wiped out, the CEO was unceremoni-
> ously dumped, and taxpayers got most
> of the upside."

The Profitable Bailout? Inside the Real Costs of the Saving AIG and Wall Street

James Kwak

*James Kwak, an associate professor at the University of Con-
necticut School of Law, is coauthor of* White House Burning:
The Founding Fathers, Our National Debt, and Why It Matters to You. *In the following viewpoint, he argues that the bailout of insurance giant American International Group Inc. (AIG)
in 2008 was very expensive but that it nonetheless was the right
thing to do. In particular, he praises the bailout for imposing punitive terms on AIG and forcing the company to reorganize. In
contrast, he says, the government was too lenient on banks and
other financial institutions at the time.*

As you read, consider the following questions:

1. According to Kwak, why did the AIG bailout cost him money?

2. Why does Kwak say the government bailout of AIG was more generous than the market would provide?

3. What does Kwak say the government should have done with JPMorgan Chase, and why?

This week [in September 2012], the Treasury Department sold another large slug of [multinational insurance company] AIG [American International Group Inc.] shares that it bought in the dark days of 2008–2009, bringing government ownership below 50 percent for the first time since the financial crisis. The deal was priced at $32.50 per share, above the $28.73 break-even price as determined by Treasury, lending support to claims by government officials that the bailouts (a) made money and (b) were a good idea. The most emphatic cheerleading came from Andrew Ross Sorkin, who declared victory for the government and quoted a White House official saying of longtime critic Neil Barofsky, "Some people just don't like movies with happy endings."

The "Good" Bailout

If only things were so simple.

First, there's the little question of Treasury's arithmetic. More importantly, AIG was in many ways the "good" bailout, where shareholders were almost wiped out, the CEO [chief executive officer] was unceremoniously dumped, and taxpayers got most of the upside. In contrast, it was the government's treatment of the biggest banks that was the travesty.

On the arithmetic: Treasury calculates a break-even price of $28.73 for the federal government's entire investment in AIG, including the emergency $85 billion line of credit extended by the Federal Reserve on September 16, 2008, and another $38 billion transaction the next month. But what happened next is that in November 2008 Treasury used TARP [Troubled Asset Relief Program] money to buy $40 billion in Series D preferred shares, giving AIG cash to pay down its credit line; in March 2009 Treasury used another $30 billion in TARP money to buy Series F preferred shares (while converting the Series D shares into Series E shares on more favorable terms to AIG), and also bought a big chunk of convertible preferred shares. . . .

Barofsky calculates a break-even price of $43.53 for TARP's investments in AIG, which Sorkin doesn't contest. This is relevant for two reasons. First, it shows that the terms of the November and March restructurings were less good for taxpayers than the terms of the original bailout. Second, if you are trying to evaluate Treasury's decision to use TARP money— which was Barofsky's job, after all, as special inspector general for TARP—$43.53 is the relevant price. If you're evaluating all federal government involvement, then arguably $28.73 is the relevant price.

But only arguably, because if you're evaluating all federal government involvement, you have to evaluate all of it— including all the cheap money that the Federal Reserve used to keep the financial system afloat and protect the value of the assets that AIG unloaded onto the . . . Federal Reserve. One consequence has been depressed rates for savers. Because I saved a lot of the money I made in my business career, negative real yields on bonds, money market funds, and savings accounts for the past three-plus years have cost me thousands if not tens of thousands of dollars. That's fine for me personally: I can afford it, and plenty of other people need money more than I do. But that money was part of the cost of shoring up AIG. More generally, you can't separate the accounting cost of the bailouts from the total costs of government policy, as brilliantly explained by Steve Randy Waldman (hat tip Yves Smith, who has additional issues with Sorkin).

Mike Baldwin, "Living Bailout to Bailout: Please Help," CartoonStock.com.

Harsh Terms

The Sorkin/Treasury vs. Barofsky spat, however, obscures the true historical place of the AIG bailout. Many administration critics, including Barofsky and including me, have always said that the Federal Reserve's emergency action on September 16 was the right thing to do, since the alternative was, at minimum, a much more destructive firestorm of panic in the financial markets. And it was done on plausibly reasonable terms. It was more generous than the market would provide (since the market wouldn't lend AIG money on any terms), but it was relatively punitive and as good for taxpayers as could be hoped. The credit line had a high interest rate, the government got 80 percent of the company, and the CEO was forced to resign. It was precisely because of those harsh terms—in particular the effective nationalization of the company—that Treasury can claim to have turned a profit on the deal.

It was what came later that I and others criticized: The use of AIG to bail out investment banks like Goldman Sachs [Group Inc.] by closing out transactions on unfavorable terms for AIG (and taxpayers); the continued payment of large bonuses to traders at AIG Financial Products; and, most importantly, the kid-glove treatment of Citigroup, Bank of America, and the other megabanks that would have collapsed were it not for government support. Unlike AIG, they were given cash on Christmas-present terms while Treasury took only a minimal amount of equity, meaning that taxpayers had all of the downside and very little upside. The CEOs, who drove their banks over the cliff and into the waiting government safety net, were allowed to keep their jobs.

At the time (early 2009), administration supporters argued that the government couldn't take majority stakes in the big banks. That would be "nationalization," which is a big, scary word that sounds kind of like "socialism." Well, we nationalized AIG, and now the company is getting universal plaudits for its performance during the period it was owned by taxpayers. JPMorgan [Chase], by contrast, keeps noticing that more billions of dollars are slipping through its pocket, and Bank of America is struggling to keep its head above water. Above all, these non-nationalized banks are still doing a lousy job extending credit to the real economy, preferring to keep their money in cash.

Tell me again what the problem with nationalization was?

> *"The key policy failure was likely regulators' decision the preceding March in favor of bailing out Bear Stearns."*

Bankruptcy Is Always Preferable to Government Bailout

Norbert J. Michel

Norbert J. Michel is a research fellow in financial regulations in the Thomas A. Roe Institute for Economic Policy Studies at the Heritage Foundation. In the following viewpoint, he argues that the failure of Lehman Brothers Holdings Inc. did not cause the financial crisis. Instead he says the crisis was caused by inconsistent government policy in regard to bailouts. The idea that failing to bail out Lehman Brothers caused the crisis is a dangerous myth, he says, because it suggests that government bailouts are a good thing rather than a huge cost to taxpayers.

As you read, consider the following questions:

1. According to Michel, when there are inconsistent government actions, what do people do?

2. To what signs of financial instability before the Lehman Brothers collapse does Michel point?

3. What does Michel say is the dangerous myth of the Lehman Brothers bailout?

September 15 [2013] marks the fifth anniversary of the Lehman Brothers [Holdings Inc.] bankruptcy, the supposed spark that set off the financial crisis of 2008. Conventional wisdom holds that it was the federal government's decision *against* bailing out this investment bank that froze credit markets and sent the economy into the "great recession." In reality, though, while the Lehman bankruptcy sent a clear signal to investors of trouble in the marketplace, it was far from the cause of the crisis.

The key policy failure was likely regulators' decision the preceding March in *favor* of bailing out Bear Stearns [Companies Inc.], a (smaller) competing investment bank, rather than the decision not to save Lehman. The Bear Stearns bailout set the expectation that Lehman would also be bailed out, setting up investors and creditors for a fall. At the very least, those with a stake in Lehman surely expected the government to minimize their losses. Thus, the inconsistent treatment of the two investment banks—not simply the act of letting Lehman file bankruptcy—was the main problem.

Arbitrary Decisions

Economists have long recognized that an inability to predict future government actions can lead people to (at best) delay their decision making. People will most likely wait to buy housing, for instance, if they are unsure what flood insurance rates the government will announce in a few months.

In the case of Lehman and Bear Stearns, two of the nation's largest investment banks, inconsistent government policy heightened uncertainty in the financial markets. On March 24,

2008, the Federal Reserve announced it would provide (through the New York Fed) special financing to "facilitate" JPMorgan Chase's acquisition of the financially troubled Bear Stearns. In other words, the U.S. government bailed out the investment bank Bear Stearns, allowing shareholders to avoid a total loss.

Naturally, the managers, creditors, shareholders, and potential buyers of Lehman Brothers (a much larger investment bank) expected similar treatment. When both Barclays [PLC] and Bank of America were unable to secure similar protection against losses, they withdrew their bids. Lehman filed for bankruptcy the next day—September 15, 2008.

It would have been inconsistent, but at least coherent, if the decision to let Lehman fail indicated that the federal government was not going to rescue any additional financial institutions. Instead, on September 16, the Federal Reserve announced it would lend (again through the New York Fed) up to $85 billion to the American International Group (AIG), an insurance company.

The AIG bailout is often blamed on "contagion" from the Lehman bankruptcy, but AIG was financially troubled well before the Fed bailed it out. Lehman's collapse, of course, did affect AIG but only because it raised real questions about the worth of AIG's assets. The problem with AIG and Lehman (as well as other firms) was that they made highly leveraged bets on assets tied to worthless mortgages. Those assets lost value not because of the Lehman bankruptcy but because the default rates on the mortgages soared. Lehman was only the messenger, not the cause, of the bad news.

The bailouts only multiplied after that. Within days of the AIG bailout, Treasury Secretary [Henry] Paulson was requesting an eye-popping $700 billion to bail out other institutions. The legislation regarding this request eventually became known as the Troubled Asset Relief Program (TARP).

Trouble Already in the Economy

Aside from the turmoil caused by the incoherent policy of the federal government, there are several other reasons that point to the Lehman bankruptcy as just one of the symptoms, rather than a cause, of the financial crisis:

- By the first quarter of 2007, defaults on subprime mortgages had risen to a four-year high. These mortgages, along with the mortgage-backed securities that were tied to them, represent the "toxic assets" that the TARP program was originally designed to get rid of.

- By the last quarter of 2007, almost exactly one year prior to the Lehman collapse, both personal consumption expenditures and civilian employment for the U.S. began downward trends.

- The difference between key interest rates spiked during the last half of 2007. The rise in these "spreads"—a commonly used measure of perceived risk—indicates that market participants saw trouble in 2007. Aside from the widely reported issues in the interbank lending markets (a short-term lending market used by banks), the spread between three-month commercial paper rates (a short-term lending market used by all sorts of people) and U.S. Treasury rates also widened in August of 2007.

- The Federal Housing Finance Agency placed Fannie Mae [the Federal National Mortgage Association] and Freddie Mac [Federal Home Loan Mortgage Corporation] in government conservatorship on September 7, 2008—one week before the Lehman bankruptcy filing.

There is little doubt that the Federal Reserve noticed the dangers well before Lehman Brothers failed. The record shows that the Federal Reserve lowered its interest rate target for the federal funds rate (another key short-term lending market for banks) from 5.25 percent in September 2007 to 3 percent in January 2008. Such an aggressive move by the Fed is highly unusual and occurs only when the Fed fears an economic downturn. The signs of fundamental trouble in the economy were clear, and they would not go away regardless of a Lehman bailout.

A Dangerous Myth

The notion that allowing Lehman to file bankruptcy caused the financial crisis is both wrong and dangerous. The danger in this myth is that it perpetuates the policy of bailing out financial institutions with taxpayer money—and that it allows policy makers who caused the crisis to escape responsibility for their actions.

Periodical and Internet Sources Bibliography

The following articles have been selected to supplement the diverse views presented in this chapter.

Mark Calabria	"Bailouts Leave a Legacy of Cronyism," *USA Today*, December 23, 2013.
Joe Deaux	"The Real Story Behind the U.S. Auto Bailouts," *Forbes*, May 5, 2012.
Sam Frizell	"General Motors Bailout Cost Taxpayers $11.2 Billion," *Time*, April 30, 2014.
John Garen	"Bankruptcy vs. Bailout?," *Business Lexington* (Kentucky), March 2, 2012.
Jennifer Liberto	"Five Years Later, TARP Price Tag Hits $40 Billion," CNN Money, April 30, 2014.
Ben Klayman	"Auto Industry Bailout an Impressive Success: Report," *Fiscal Times*, December 9, 2013.
Brian O'Connell	"Did the Fed Bank Bailout Work After All?," TheStreet, June 13, 2014.
Andrew Ross Sorkin	"What Might Have Been, and the Fall of Lehman," *New York Times*, September 9, 2013.
USA Today	"Report: GM Bailout Saved 1.2 Million Jobs," December 9, 2013.
Peter Weber	"The U.S. Auto Bailout Is Officially Over. Here's What America Lost and Gained," *The Week*, December 10, 2013.
David Weidner	"TARP: The Bailout Success Story That Wasn't," MarketWatch, February 12, 2013.

For Further Discussion

Chapter 1

1. After reading the viewpoints in this chapter, what is your opinion on bankruptcy? Do you think it's immoral, or do you think it's a way to clear up debt and start on a path toward financial stability? Use examples from the viewpoints to support your answer.

2. Paul Ritz points out the hidden dangers of declaring bankruptcy. What are the dangers the author cites? Which of these dangers do you think are the most serious, and why?

3. Leonora Gorelik argues that filing for bankruptcy in one's twenties or thirties may be beneficial. Do you agree with the author? Why, or why not?

Chapter 2

1. Devon Merling asserts that bankruptcy laws should be changed to include discharge of student loans. In what ways does the author believe this would help those who declare bankruptcy? Do you agree with the author's argument? Why, or why not?

2. Matthew Stein argues that the Patient Protection and Affordable Care Act, or Obamacare, will help save self-employed people from medical bankruptcy. Conversely, Sarah Kliff claims that Obamacare will not necessarily end medical bankruptcies. With which author do you agree, and why?

Chapter 3

1. As Jim Christie reports, Stockton, California, was able to negotiate with its creditors and reduce its liabilities while retaining public employees' pensions. How was the city

able to accomplish this? Do you think this strategy could work for other cities as well? Explain your reasoning.

2. Ariana Eunjung Cha maintains that Vallejo, California, has rebounded since declaring bankruptcy, while Melanie Hicken claims that the city is still struggling financially. What evidence does each author provide to support her argument? Which author do you think presents the better case? Explain.

Chapter 4

1. After reading the viewpoints in this chapter, do you think the US government bailouts of the banking system and automobile industry were needed during the 2008 financial crisis, or should the government not have intervened? Explain your reasoning, and use examples from the viewpoints to support your answer.

2. Erik Larson asserts that the Lehman Brothers bankruptcy was a success. What are some examples the author gives for this reasoning? In your opinion, should Lehman Brothers have been bailed out like some other financial institutions were? Explain.

3. Norbert J. Michel concludes that the financial crisis was caused by inconsistent government policy on bailouts, not by the failure of Lehman Brothers. Based on the evidence in the viewpoint, do you agree or disagree with the author, and why?

Organizations to Contact

The editors have compiled the following list of organizations concerned with the issues debated in this book. The descriptions are derived from materials provided by the organizations. All have publications or information available for interested readers. The list was compiled on the date of publication of the present volume; the information provided here may change. Be aware that many organizations take several weeks or longer to respond to inquiries, so allow as much time as possible.

American Bankruptcy Institute (ABI)
66 Canal Center Plaza, Suite 600, Alexandria, VA 22314
(703) 739-0800 • fax: (703) 739-1060
e-mail: support@abiworld.org
website: www.abiworld.org

The American Bankruptcy Institute (ABI) is dedicated to research and education on bankruptcy issues. ABI provides information to journalists and policy makers, as well as offers bankruptcy education to consumers. Its website includes a Consumer Bankruptcy Center that offers information about bankruptcy, a question-and-answer section, and referrals to attorneys. ABI publishes the *ABI Journal* and the *ABI Update* newsletter. Additionally, its website offers a blog with entries such as "I Have One Huge Medical Debt. Is Bankruptcy the Answer?" and "Why Bankruptcy May Be the Answer to Your Student Loan Problems."

Center for Responsible Lending (CRL)
302 West Main Street, Durham, NC 27701
(919) 313-8500
website: www.responsiblelending.org

The Center for Responsible Lending (CRL) is a nonprofit, nonpartisan research and policy organization dedicated to protecting family wealth by working to eliminate abusive financial practices that can lead to bankruptcy. CRL has conducted and commissioned landmark studies on predatory lending practices and the impact of state laws that protect borrowers. It also lobbies Congress in favor of laws to reform harmful lending practices. CRL publishes many resources for consumers, including fact sheets, testimony, and articles such as "Payday Loans: A Stepping Stone to Debt, Reduced Credit Options and Bankruptcy."

Consumer Action (CA)

221 Main Street, Suite 480, San Francisco, CA 94105
(415) 777-9635 • fax: (415) 777-5267
website: www.consumer-action.org

Consumer Action (CA) is a nonprofit organization that was founded in San Francisco in 1971 to protect and advance the rights of consumers. During its more than four decades, Consumer Action has served consumers nationwide through advocacy, education, and outreach. It manned one of the country's first consumer hotlines, which today receives more than seven hundred calls and e-mails each month. Among its many publications, including its consumer newspaper *Consumer Action News* and its e-newsletter *Consumer Action Insider*, are fact sheets, articles, reports, and brochures such as "Bankruptcy: Your Right to a Financial Fresh Start."

Debtors Anonymous (DA)

PO Box 920888, Needham, MA 02492-0009
(781) 453-2743 • fax: (781) 453-2745
e-mail: office@debtorsanonymous.org
website: www.debtorsanonymous.org

Modeled upon Alcoholics Anonymous, Debtors Anonymous (DA) is a twelve-step spiritual self-help program that aims to end the cycle of debt. The DA website provides information on what a compulsive debtor is and how a compulsive debtor can get help and offers guidance on finding and conducting meetings. The website also offers personal stories of success from some of DA's thousands of members. DA publishes pamphlets, books, and the *Ways and Means* newsletter.

Economic Policy Institute (EPI)
1333 H Street NW, Suite 300, East Tower
Washington, DC 20005
(202) 775-8810 • fax: (202) 775-0819
e-mail: epi@epi.org
website: www.epi.org

The Economic Policy Institute (EPI) is a nonprofit, nonpartisan Washington-based think tank created in 1986 to include the needs of low- and middle-income Americans in economic policy discussions. EPI believes every working person deserves a good job with fair pay, affordable health care, and retirement security. Each year, EPI publishes "The State of Working America" report, which analyzes the US economy's impact on the living standards of working families. The EPI website includes articles, such as "In over Our Heads—Debt Burdens, Bankruptcies on the Rise," and the *Working Economics* blog.

Hoover Institution
434 Galvez Mall, Stanford University
Stanford, CA 94305-6010
(650) 723-1754 • fax: (650) 723-1687
website: www.hoover.org

Founded in 1919 by future president Herbert Hoover, the Hoover Institution is a public policy research center. It publishes the *Hoover Daily Report*, the quarterly *Hoover Digest*, and the online journal *Defining Ideas*, as well as articles, reports, and working papers. Its website features links to several blogs in which its scholars contribute with posts such as "Why Bankruptcy Is the Best Solution for American Auto Companies" and "Should States Be Allowed to Declare Bankruptcy?"

Jump$tart Coalition for Personal Financial Literacy
919 Eighteenth Street NW, Suite 300, Washington, DC 20006
(888) 45-EDUCATE • fax: (202) 223-0321
e-mail: info@jumpstartcoalition.org
website: www.jumpstartcoalition.org

Dedicated to improving the financial literacy of kindergarten through college-age youth, Jump$tart provides advocacy, research, and educational resources to students. Jump$tart's website offers tools such as the Reality Check test designed to teach students what they will need to accomplish to reach their financial goals. The website also provides a clearinghouse of financial education resources for teachers, parents, and caregivers, as well as downloadable publications. Jump$tart publishes the quarterly newsletter *Jump$tart Update*.

National Association of Consumer Advocates (NACA)
1730 Rhode Island Avenue NW, Suite 710
Washington, DC   20036
(202) 452-1989 • fax: (202) 452-0099
e-mail: info@naca.net
website: http://naca.net

The National Association of Consumer Advocates (NACA) is a nonprofit association that promotes justice for all consumers. Made up of more than fifteen hundred attorneys and advocates, the NACA fights for consumer rights by lobbying policy makers, drafting legislation, and advocating on behalf of consumers on a variety of issues, including bankruptcy, predatory lending practices, and debt collection abuse. NACA's blog, *The Consumer Advocate*, can be found at its website.

National Bureau of Economic Research (NBER)
1050 Massachusetts Avenue, Cambridge, MA   02138
(617) 868-3900
e-mail: info@nber.org
website: www.nber.org

Founded in 1920, the National Bureau of Economic Research (NBER) is a private, nonprofit, nonpartisan research organization that undertakes unbiased economic research among public policy makers, business professionals, and the academic community. A search of the NBER website produces numerous working papers and other information on various economic issues. Examples of recent publications include "Mortgage Default, Foreclosure and Bankruptcy" and "Bankruptcy: Past Puzzles, Recent Reforms, and the Mortgage Crisis."

National Consumer Law Center (NCLC)

7 Winthrop Square, Boston, MA   02110-1245
(617) 542-8010 • fax: (617) 542-8028
e-mail: consumerlaw@nclc.org
website: www.nclc.org

The National Consumer Law Center (NCLC) is a nonprofit organization that works for consumer justice and economic security for low-income and disadvantaged people in the United States. NCLC works with nonprofit and legal services organizations, private attorneys, policy makers, and federal and state government and courts across the nation to stop exploitative practices and help financially stressed families build and retain wealth. The NCLC offers a database of lawyers across the United States who specialize in consumer issues such as personal bankruptcy. The NCLC website features a For Consumers section that offers guides, brochures, fact sheets, and articles such as "Answers to Common Bankruptcy Questions."

National Endowment for Financial Education (NEFE)

1331 Seventeenth Street, Suite 1200, Denver, CO   80202
(303) 741-6333
website: www.nefe.org

The National Endowment for Financial Education (NEFE) is a national nonprofit organization that seeks to improve the financial well-being of Americans. It offers materials for educators, research for consumers, and tips for financial planning and money-management assistance. NEFE's High School Financial Planning program introduces young adults to basic personal finance practices to help them build sensible money management skills. NEFE's Smart About Money program educates Americans on a broad range of topics and empowers individuals to make sound decisions to reach their financial goals. It offers the bimonthly *NEFE Digest*.

National Foundation for Credit Counseling (NFCC)
2000 M Street NW, Suite 505, Washington, DC 20036
(202) 677-4300
website: www.nfcc.org

The nation's largest nonprofit credit counseling network, the National Foundation for Credit Counseling (NFCC) works to provide counseling services to consumers in need of financial advice. The NFCC offers help in finding credit and bankruptcy counselors; provides consumers with financial education materials, including budget worksheets and online debt calculators; and hosts national financial education initiatives such as the National Protect Your Identity Week. The NFCC website provides consumer tips, podcasts, videos, and a blog, *Stay the Course*, which includes articles such as "Recovering from Bankruptcy" and "Bankruptcy: What You Need to Know Before You File."

Bibliography of Books

Mandy Akridge   *Negotiate and Settle Your Debts: A
                    Debt Settlement Strategy.* Seattle, WA:
                    CreateSpace, 2011.

Neil Barofsky   *Bailout: How Washington Abandoned
                    Main Street While Rescuing Wall
                    Street.* New York: Free Press, 2012.

Nathan Beck   *Bankruptcy: Chapter 11 Bankruptcy
                    Blueprint: Successfully Navigate
                    Chapter 11 Bankruptcy with Complete
                    Confidence.* Louisville, KY: Afflatus
                    Publishing, 2014.

Alane A. Becket   *Consumer Bankruptcy: Fundamentals
and William A.   of Chapter 7 and Chapter 13 of the
McNeal   U.S. Bankruptcy Code.* 3rd ed.
                    Alexandria, VA: American
                    Bankruptcy Institute, 2011.

Bethany   *Bailout!: Government Intervention in
Bezdecheck   Business.* New York: Rosen
                    Publishing, 2010.

Brian A. Blum   *Bankruptcy and Debtor/Creditor:
                    Examples & Explanations.* 5th ed.
                    New York: Aspen Publishers, 2010.

Stephen Elias   *The Foreclosure Survival Guide: Keep
                    Your House or Walk Away with
                    Money in Your Pocket.* 3rd ed.
                    Berkeley, CA: Nolo Press, 2011.

Stephen Elias and   *How to File for Chapter 7 Bankruptcy.*
Albin Renauer   18th ed. Berkeley, CA: Nolo Press,
                    2013.

Stephen Elias and Kathleen Michon	*Chapter 13 Bankruptcy: Keep Your Property & Repay Debts over Time.* 11th ed. Berkeley, CA: Nolo Press, 2012.
Stephen Elias and Leon Bayer	*The New Bankruptcy: Will It Work for You?* 5th ed. Berkeley, CA: Nolo Press, 2013.
Christopher Forrest	*The Strategic Default Plan: How to Walk Away from Your Mortgage.* Seattle, WA: CreateSpace, 2012.
William C. Hillman and Margaret M. Crouch	*Personal Bankruptcy Answer Book.* New York: Practising Law Institute, 2010.
Robin Leonard and Margaret Reiter	*Solve Your Money Troubles: Debt, Credit and Bankruptcy.* 14th ed. Berkeley, CA: Nolo Press, 2013.
Nathalie Martin	*The Glannon Guide to Bankruptcy: Learning Bankruptcy Through Multiple-Choice Questions and Analysis.* 3rd ed. New York: Aspen Publishers, 2011.
Adam Palmer	*Personal Bankruptcy: What to Do When Faced with Bankruptcy and How to File for Chapter 7.* New York: BMS Publishing, 2014.
Katherine Porter	*Broke: How Debt Bankrupts the Middle Class.* Stanford, CA: Stanford University Press, 2012.
Jerry Robinson	*Bankruptcy of Our Nation.* Green Forest, AR: New Leaf Press, 2012.

Adam Rudeen — *Personal Bankruptcy: Fully Rebuild Your Credit Stress Free in 2 Years While Avoiding an Emotional Bankruptcy.* Huntsville, AL: Fluency Books, 2014.

Wendell Schollander and Wes Schollander — *The Personal Bankruptcy Answer Book: Practical Answers to More than 175 Questions on Bankruptcy.* Naperville, IL: Sphinx, 2009.

Andrew Ross Sorkin — *Too Big to Fail: The Inside Story of How Wall Street and Washington Fought to Save the Financial System—and Themselves.* New York: Penguin, 2010.

Gary H. Stern and Ron J. Feldman — *Too Big to Fail: The Hazards of Bank Bailouts.* Washington, DC: Brookings Institution Press, 2009.

Stuart Vyse — *Going Broke: Why Americans Can't Hold On to Their Money.* New York: Oxford University Press, 2008.

Brent T. White — *Underwater Home: What Should You Do if You Owe More on Your Home than It's Worth?* Seattle, WA: CreateSpace, 2010.

Robert E. Wright — *Bailouts: Public Money, Private Profit.* New York: Columbia University Press, 2010.

Index

F

Fabian, Matt, 80

Fairness for Struggling Students Act (bill), 55

Farmer, Liz, 101

Federal bailouts, pension shortfalls, 88, 92

Federal courts of appeals, 52–55

Federal Deposit Insurance Corporation (FDIC), 138, 139–140

Federal funding, colleges and universities, 46

Federal funds rate, 150–151

Federal Home Loan Mortgage Corporation (Freddie Mac), 61, 133, 150

Federal National Mortgage Association (Fannie Mae), 61, 133, 150

Federal Reserve. *See* US Federal Reserve

Federal Reserve Bank of New York, 15, 47, 63

Federal Reserve Board, 110, 114, 133, 137, 138–139

Ferrell, Linda, 134

Ferrell, O.C., 134

Fiat S.p.A., 126

Filing for bankruptcy
costs, 14–15, 27
decisions, 27, 30, 32
documentation collection, 43–44
frequency, laws, 33–34, 34–35
processes and challenges, 31
time needed to file, 16
young people (20s and 30s), 36–40

Financial Crisis Inquiry Commission (FCIC), 138–139

Financial crisis of 2008. *See* Global financial crisis, 2008

Financial industry
bailout decisions and packages, 133, 138, 139, 142–146, 148–151
bailouts by the numbers, 127*t*
Lehman Brothers bailout support, 137–141
Lehman Brothers bankruptcy, 129–136

Financial Peace University, 30–31, 33

Ford Motor Company, 109, 110–111, 113, 120, 126, 128

Foreclosures
aid to foreclosed, 57, 59, 63
links to bankruptcy reform, 15
rates, and lack of help to homeowners, 57, 59

Forgiveness of debt. *See* Debt forgiveness

Fraedrich, John, 134

Frates, Steven, 87

Fraud, 28, 43

Free market values, 113–114

Fuel-efficiency standards, 118

Fulwiler, Joe, 29–35

G

Galbraith, Alison, 76–77

Gasoline prices, 118

Geithner, Tim, 119

General Motors (GM), 109, 110–120, 121, 124, 126

Gingrich, Newt, 125

Global financial crisis, 2008, 65, 106
automobile industry and bailouts, 108–109

US Federal Reserve
  economic health monitoring,
    150–151
  financial industry bailouts and
    decisions, 110, 133, 137,
    138–139, 140, 143–146, 148–
    149
  rates, 150–151
US Supreme Court, 49

V

Vacaville, California, 97
Valenti, Joe, 47, 48, 50
Vallejo, California
  bankruptcy, 86–87, 90, 93,
    95–96, 100–101, 102–103
  recovery, 93–98
  still can't afford pensions, 99–
    103
Valukas, Anton, 139–140
Volunteer crime reporting, 96–97,
  102

W

Wagoner, Rick, 116
Waldman, Steve Randy, 144
Wallison, Peter J., 137–141
Weil, Gotshal & Manges LLP, 130,
  132, 135–136
White, Michelle J., 14–15
Whitney, Meredith, 95
Whittom, Craig, 98
Woolhandler, Stephanie, 75–76

Y

Young Americans. *See* Thirty-
somethings; Twenty-somethings

Z

Zellers, Russell, 102
Zywicki, Todd J., 62–67